WORLD WAR II

History SparkNotes

Spark Publishing
A Division of Barnes & Noble Publishing
120 Fifth Avenue
New York, NY 10011
www.sparknotes.com

ISBN-13: 978-1-4114-0428-1
ISBN-10: 1-4114-0428-9

Library of Congress information available upon request.

Please submit changes or report errors to www.sparknotes.com/errors.

Printed and bound in the United States.

1 3 5 7 9 10 8 6 4 2

CONTENTS

OVERVIEW

World War II effectively stopped the world between 1939 and 1945. To this day, it remains the most geographically widespread military conflict the world has ever seen. Although the fighting reached across many parts of the globe, most countries involved shared a united effort aimed at ending the aggression of the Axis Powers—Germany, Italy, and Japan. Despite the fact that Germany and Japan were technically allies, however, they had vastly different motives and objectives, and their level of cooperation was primarily one of distracting the attention of each other's enemies rather than of attaining any specific common goals. Therefore, most studies of the war cover the conflicts with Germany and Japan separately, dividing treatment of the war between the European and Pacific theaters of operation.

The rise of Nazi Germany and its aggression can be traced directly back to World War I. Following that war, Germany was economically devastated. The Treaty of Versailles unfairly placed the full blame for the war on Germany and demanded heavy reparations payments in return. Although Germany never paid the bulk of these reparations, the treaty humiliated the German people and obstructed the nation's efforts to rebuild itself and move forward economically and technologically. Then, in the late 1920s and early 1930s, the worldwide Great Depression took a further heavy toll on the country.

As resentment and desperation in Germany grew, radical political parties gained in popularity. They ranged from Communists to right-wing nationalists. Among the more extreme activists of the latter category was Adolf Hitler, who had founded the National Socialist German Workers' Party (more commonly known as the Nazi Party) in 1920–1921. By the time of the depression in Germany, Hitler's party had more than 100,000 members and was growing rapidly, and it began participating in parliamentary elections with increasing success. In 1933, Hitler pressured the German president, Paul von Hindenburg, into appointing him chancellor—a position from which he was quickly able to consolidate his power.

By 1935, Germany had ceased to recognize the Treaty of Versailles and all the restrictions that accompanied it. In particular, Hitler announced his intention to fully rebuild Germany's military forces. In 1938, Germany began annexing the territories of neighboring countries, including all of Austria and most of Czechoslovakia. When Germany attacked Poland in September 1939, Britain and France aligned against Germany, and the war began.

Like Germany, Japan was severely affected by the Great Depression. Japan relied heavily upon imported resources and desperately needed more land for its expanding population. Japanese military leaders, who at the time had a strong influence over the civilian government, saw territorial expansion as the best solution. As a result, beginning in 1931, Japanese forces began occupying territory in the Chinese region of Manchuria. By 1937, Japan and China were officially at war. In 1940, the Japanese government announced its intention to establish a "new order in East Asia," under which the region would be freed of Western influence and guided by Japan. In 1940, Japan signed a formal alliance with Germany and Italy, setting the country on a clear course to enter World War II.

In the meantime, the United States, disapproving of Japan's actions, placed a heavy trade embargo on Japan, severely restricting its ability to import oil, scrap metal, and other resources vital to its war effort. Japan saw itself facing an impossible crisis, and without prompt and decisive action, total collapse was inevitable. The action Japan chose was a surprise attack on the U.S. naval base at Pearl Harbor, Hawaii, on December 7, 1941. This action brought the United States into World War II in both theaters, Europe and the Pacific.

Summary of Events

The European Theater

German Aggression

The war in Europe began in September 1939, when Germany, under Chancellor **Adolf Hitler**, invaded **Poland**. Britain and France responded by declaring war on Germany but took little action over the following months. In 1940, Germany launched its next initiative by attacking **Denmark** and **Norway**, followed shortly thereafter by attacks on **Belgium**, the **Netherlands**, and **France**. All of these nations were conquered rapidly.

The Battle of Britain

Later in the summer of 1940, Germany launched a further attack on **Britain**, this time exclusively from the air. The **Battle of Britain** was Germany's first military failure, as the German air force, the **Luftwaffe**, was never able to overcome Britain's Royal Air Force.

Greece and North Africa

As Hitler plotted his next steps, **Italy**, an ally of Germany, expanded the war even further by invading **Greece** and **North Africa**. The Greek campaign was a failure, and Germany was forced to come to Italy's assistance in early 1941.

The USSR

Later in 1941, Germany began its most ambitious action yet, by invading the **Soviet Union**. Although the Germans initially made swift progress and advanced deep into the Russian heartland, the invasion of the USSR would prove to be the downfall of Germany's war effort. The country was just too big, and although Russia's initial resistance was weak, the nation's strength and determination, combined with its brutal winters, would eventually be more than the German army could overcome. In 1943, after the battles of **Stalingrad** and **Kursk**, Germany was forced into a full-scale retreat. During the course of 1944, the Germans were slowly but steadily forced completely out of Soviet territory, after which the Russians pursued them across eastern Europe and into Germany itself in 1945.

THE NORMANDY INVASION

In June 1944, British and American forces launched the **D-Day invasion**, landing in German-occupied France via the coast of **Normandy**. Soon the German army was forced into retreat from that side as well. Thus, by early 1945, Allied forces were closing in on Germany from both east and west. The Soviets were the first to reach the German capital of **Berlin**, and Germany surrendered in May 1945, shortly after the suicide of Adolf Hitler.

THE PACIFIC THEATER

PEARL HARBOR

The war in the Pacific began on December 7, 1941, when warplanes from **Japan** launched a surprise attack on the U.S. Navy base at **Pearl Harbor**, Hawaii. By this time, Japan had already been at war with **China** for several years and had seized the Chinese territory of **Manchuria**. After the Pearl Harbor attack, Japan began a massive campaign of expansion throughout the Southeast Asia–Pacific region.

THE U.S. ENTRANCE AND BATTLE OF MIDWAY

Although the Pearl Harbor attack provoked a declaration of war by the **United States** on Japan the very next day, it would be several months before U.S. forces would get seriously involved militarily. In late spring of 1942, the United States and Japan engaged in a series of naval battles, climaxing in the **Battle of Midway** on June 3–6, 1942, in which Japan suffered a catastrophic defeat.

THE SOLOMON ISLANDS AND GUADALCANAL

For the next year, the United States engaged Japan in a protracted struggle for the **Solomon Islands**, which lay near vital Allied shipping routes. Between August 1942 and February 1943, Allied forces carried out an invasion on the island of **Guadalcanal**—the beginning of a long series of Allied offensives that would eventually force the Japanese out of the Solomons and then pursue them from various other Pacific island chains that the Japanese had earlier seized. In the meantime, British and Indian forces were combating Japanese troops in **Burma**.

THE APPROACH TO JAPAN

Fighting continued throughout the Pacific in 1944 and early 1945, including major battles at **Leyte**, **Iwo Jima**, and **Okinawa**. By the late spring of 1945, most of Japan's conquests had been liberated, and Allied forces were closing in on the Japanese home islands. As they neared Japan proper, the Allies began heavy bombing campaigns against major Japanese cities, including **Tokyo**. This process continued through the summer of 1945 until finally, in early August, the United States dropped two **atomic bombs** on the cities of **Hiroshima** and **Nagasaki**. Stunned by the unexpected devastation, Japan surrendered a few days later.

KEY PEOPLE & TERMS

PEOPLE

NEVILLE CHAMBERLAIN
The prime minister of Britain from 1937 to 1940, who advocated a policy of **appeasement** toward the territorial demands of Nazi **Germany**. This appeasement policy essentially turned a blind eye to Germany's 1938 annexation of **Austria** and the **Sudetenland**.

WINSTON CHURCHILL
The prime minister of Britain during most of World War II. Churchill was among the most active leaders in resisting German aggression and played a major role in assembling the **Allied Powers**, including the United States and the USSR.

JAMES DOOLITTLE
A U.S. Army general best known for leading the famous **"Doolittle Raid"** in 1942, in which B-25 bombers were launched from an aircraft carrier to bomb **Japan** and then crash-landed in **China**.

DWIGHT D. EISENHOWER
A U.S. Army general who held the position of supreme Allied commander in Europe, among many others. Eisenhower was perhaps best known for his work in planning **Operation Overlord**, the Allied invasion of Europe. After the war, he was a very popular figure in the United States and was elected to two terms as U.S. president, taking office in 1953.

HIROHITO
Emperor of **Japan** from 1926 until his death in 1989. Despite the power of Japan's military leaders, many scholars believe that Hirohito took an active role in leading the country and shaping its combat strategy during World War II. After Japan's defeat, he was allowed to continue to hold his position as emperor—largely as a figurehead—despite the fact that Japan was under U.S. occupation. Although many countries favored it, Hirohito was never tried for war crimes.

ADOLF HITLER

Chancellor and self-proclaimed **Führer**, or "leader," of **Germany** from 1933 until his suicide in 1945. After a rapid political ascent as the leader of the far-right **Nazi Party** in the 1920s, Hitler achieved absolute power and maintained it throughout his time as chancellor. During his rule, he took a very active role in the government of Germany, making military decisions and implementing edicts regarding the treatment of Jews and other minorities, such as the notorious **"final solution"** that condemned Jews to death at **concentration camps** in German-controlled parts of Europe. Just before Germany surrendered in 1945, Hitler committed suicide together with his wife, **Eva Braun**, in his bunker in Berlin.

YAMAMOTO ISOROKU

The Japanese navy admiral who planned the surprise attack on **Pearl Harbor** in 1941 and the attack on **Midway** in 1942.

CURTIS LEMAY

The commander of the U.S. Air Force's 21st Bomber Command in the Pacific theater during World War II. LeMay is best known for developing the U.S. strategy of using massive incendiary bomb attacks on Japanese cities in order to break the Japanese will near the end of the war.

BENITO MUSSOLINI

Fascist prime minister who came to power in 1922 and ruled Italy as an absolute dictator. In many ways, Mussolini served as an inspiration to **Adolf Hitler**, with whom he chose to ally himself during World War II. In 1943, Mussolini was overthrown in a coup orchestrated by some of his subordinates, and in 1945 he was executed by Italian partisans just prior to the end of the war in Europe.

FRIEDRICH PAULUS

A field marshal in command of the German Sixth Army at the **Battle of Stalingrad**. Paulus surrendered what was left of the German forces in February 1943, despite Chancellor **Adolf Hitler**'s express orders not to do so. While a prisoner of war in the USSR, Paulus publicly condemned Hitler's regime.

ERWIN ROMMEL

A field marshal in the German army's Afrika Korps who specialized in tank warfare. Rommel came to be known by both friends and enemies as the "Desert Fox" for his brilliant strategies and surprise attacks in Germany's **North Africa** campaign.

FRANKLIN DELANO ROOSEVELT

The 32nd U.S. president, who led the country through the bulk of World War II until his death from a cerebral hemorrhage in April 1945, just a few months before the war ended. Together with **Winston Churchill** and **Joseph Stalin**, Roosevelt played a decisive role in holding together the Allied coalition that ultimately defeated Nazi Germany.

JOSEPH STALIN

General secretary of the Communist Party of the Soviet Union from 1922 until his death in 1953. In some ways, Stalin was responsible for the USSR's severe losses at the beginning of World War II, as he failed to head the warnings of his advisors and did not allow the Russian military to prepare a proper defense. At the same time, he did succeed in holding the country together and inspiring among his people an awesome resistance against **Germany**, which ultimately forced a German retreat. Stalin's own regime in the USSR was just as brutal as the Nazi regime in many ways, and the alliance between Stalin and the Western Allies always remained rather tenuous because of mutual distrust.

HARRY S TRUMAN

The 33rd U.S. president, who succeeded **Franklin D. Roosevelt** upon Roosevelt's death in April 1945. Truman, who led the country through the last few months of World War II, is best known for making the controversial decision to use two **atomic bombs** against Japan in August 1945. After the war, Truman was crucial in the implementation of the **Marshall Plan**, which greatly accelerated Western Europe's economic recovery.

TERMS

ALLIED POWERS

An alliance during World War II made up of the countries that opposed the aggression of Nazi Germany. **Britain, France**, the **United States**, and the **Soviet Union** were the most prominent members, although many other countries also joined.

ANSCHLUSS

Chancellor **Adolf Hitler**'s doctrine of German political union with **Austria,** which effectively enabled Germany to annex that nation in March 1938.

APPEASEMENT

The British and French policy of conceding to **Adolf Hitler**'s territorial demands prior to the outbreak of World War II. Associated primarily with British prime minister **Neville Chamberlain,** the appeasement policy enabled Hitler to systematically take over the territories of several neighboring countries.

AXIS POWERS

The collective term for **Germany, Italy,** and **Japan**'s military alliance in opposition to the **Allied Powers.** Several smaller countries in Eastern Europe also became members of the Axis Powers temporarily.

BATTLE OF BRITAIN

An extended campaign from July 1940 to the spring of 1941 in which British **air forces** fought off wave after wave of German bombers and denied Germany in its quest to attain air superiority over Britain. Although major cities in England sustained heavy damage, the British resistance forced Germany to abandon its plans to invade across the English Channel.

BATTLE OF THE CORAL SEA

A battle from May 4–8, 1942, in which U.S. naval forces successfully protected the Allied base at Port Moresby, **New Guinea,** the last Allied outpost standing between the Japanese onslaught and **Australia.** The battle, which caused heavy losses on both sides, was the first naval battle in history fought exclusively in the air, by carrier-based planes.

BATTLE OF EL-ALAMEIN

An October and November 1942 battle that was the climax of the North African campaign. A resounding victory by the British over the Germans, the battle paved the way for the Allied takeover of North Africa and the retreat of German forces back across the Mediterranean.

BATTLE OF GUADALCANAL

A campaign from August 1942 to February 1943 in which U.S. Marines fought brutal battles to expel Japanese forces from the **Solomon Islands,** a strategically important island chain in the South Pacific near Australia.

BATTLE OF IWO JIMA

A battle in February and March 1945 in which U.S. forces took Iwo Jima, a small but strategically important island off the Japanese coast. During the battle, an Associated Press photographer took a world-famous photograph of U.S. Marines raising the American flag on the summit of **Mt. Suribachi**.

BATTLE OF MIDWAY

A battle from June 3–6, 1942, in which U.S. naval forces severely disabled the Japanese fleet at **Midway Island** in the Pacific. Coming close on the heels of the **Battle of the Coral Sea**, the Battle of Midway forced Japan into defensive mode and turned the tide of the war in the Pacific theater.

BATTLE OF OKINAWA

The last large-scale battle in the Pacific theater, in which U.S. forces invaded the Japanese home island of Okinawa. The battle was very bloody, killing at least 100,000 Japanese soldiers and 80,000 to 100,000 Japanese civilians.

BATTLE OF STALINGRAD

A brutal, five-month battle between German and Soviet forces for the important industrial city of Stalingrad that resulted in the deaths of almost 2 million people. The battle involved very destructive air raids by the German **Luftwaffe** and bloody urban street fighting. In February 1943, despite direct orders from Hitler forbidding it, Field Marshal **Friedrich Paulus** surrendered the German forces to the Red Army.

BLITZKRIEG

Literally "lightning war," the term for Hitler's invasion strategy of attacking a nation suddenly and with overwhelming force. Hitler applied the blitzkrieg strategy, with varying degrees of success, to the German invasions of **Poland, France,** and the **Soviet Union**.

D-DAY

June 6, 1944, the day on which the Allied invasion of France via the **Normandy** coast began.

FASCISM

A system of government dominated by far-right-wing forces and generally commanded by a single dictator. Several Fascist governments were established in Europe in the early twentieth century, most notably those led by dictators **Adolf Hitler** of Germany, **Benito Mussolini** of Italy, and **Francisco Franco** of Spain.

"Final Solution"

The Nazi's euphemistic term for their plan to exterminate the **Jews** of Germany and other German-controlled territories during World War II. The term was used at the **Wannsee Conference** of January 1942, in which Nazi leaders planned the Holocaust but made no specific mention of the **extermination camps** that ultimately killed millions.

Gestapo

The brutal Nazi secret police force, headed by the infamous **Hermann Göring**. The Gestapo was responsible for the relocation of many European Jews to Nazi **concentration camps** during the war.

Lebensraum

Literally "living space," **Adolf Hitler**'s justification for Germany's aggressive territorial conquests in the late 1930s. Based on the work of a previous German ethnographer, Hitler used the idea of *lebensraum* to claim that the German people's "natural" territory extended beyond the current borders of Germany and that Germany therefore needed to acquire additional territory in Europe.

Luftwaffe

The German air force, which was used heavily in campaigns such as the **Battle of Britain** in 1940.

Manhattan Project

The code name for the U.S. government's secret program to develop an **atomic bomb**. Begun in 1942, the Manhattan Project utilized the expertise of world-famous physicists, including Albert Einstein and Enrico Fermi, to develop the weapon. It finally succeeded in conducting the first successful atomic bomb test in July 1945 at Alamogordo, New Mexico. After a difficult decision by President **Harry S Truman**, U.S. forces dropped two atomic bombs on the Japanese cities of **Hiroshima** and **Nagasaki** in August 1945, prompting Japan's surrender.

Munich Agreement

A September 30, 1938, agreement among Germany, Britain, Italy, and France that allowed Germany to annex the region of western Czechoslovakia called the **Sudetenland**. The Munich Agreement was the most famous example of British prime minister **Neville Chamberlain**'s policy of **appeasement** prior to World War II.

OPERATION BARBAROSSA

The code name for the German invasion of the **Soviet Union** in 1941, which Hitler predicted would take only six months but ended up miring the German armies for more than two years.

OPERATION OVERLORD

The code name for the Allied invasion of **France** in 1944, which commenced on the beaches of **Normandy** and ultimately was successful in liberating France and pushing German forces back east to their own territory.

S.S.

In German, *Schutzstaffel* ("protection detachment"), the elite German paramilitary unit. Originally formed as a unit to serve as Hitler's personal bodyguards, the S.S. grew and took on the duties of an elite military formation. During World War II, the Nazi regime used the S.S. to handle the extermination of Jews and other racial minorities, among other duties. The S.S. had its own army, independent of the regular German army (the **Wehrmacht**), to carry out its operations behind enemy lines.

V-E DAY

May 8, 1945, the day on which the Allied forces declared victory in Europe.

V-J DAY

August 15, 1945, the day on which the Allied forces declared victory over Japan.

WANNSEE CONFERENCE

A January 1942 conference during which Nazi officials decided to implement the **"final solution"** to the "Jewish question"—a euphemism for the extermination of European Jews and other minorities at **concentration camps** in eastern Europe.

WEHRMACHT

The term used for regular German army.

SUMMARY & ANALYSIS

THE START OF THE WAR

EVENTS

March 13, 1938	Germany annexes Austria
October 7–10	Germany takes Czech region of Sudetenland
August 23, 1939	German-Soviet Nonaggression Pact
September 1	Germany invades Poland
September 3	Britain and France declare war on Germany
September 17	USSR invades Poland from the east
September 19	German and Soviet forces meet in central Poland
September 28	Warsaw falls to Germany
November 30	Soviet forces invade Finland

KEY PEOPLE

Adolf Hitler	Chancellor of Germany; pursued aggressive territorial expansion in the late 1930s
Neville Chamberlain	British prime minister; adhered to policy of appeasement that allowed German territorial annexations in 1938
Joachim von Ribbentrop	German foreign minister; signed German-Soviet Nonaggression Pact
Vyacheslav Molotov	Soviet foreign minister; signed German-Soviet Nonaggression Pact

GERMANY UNDER HITLER

In 1938, **Germany** was a total dictatorship under the **Nazi Party** and Chancellor **Adolf Hitler**. Although the 1919 **Treaty of Versailles** that ended World War I had imposed strict disarmament terms on Germany, by the late 1930s, Hitler had dropped all pretense of observing the terms of the treaty. He began not only to rebuild his military rapidly, but also to speak openly of Germany's need for *lebensraum*, or "living space."

ANSCHLUSS AND APPEASEMENT

In March 1938, offering little in the way of justification, Nazi troops took control **Austria**, which put up no resistance. Hitler claimed that the annexation was supported by his doctrine of *Anschluss*, or natural political unification of Germany and Austria. Though gravely disturbed, Britain and France took no action. Shortly thereafter, Hitler demanded that Czechoslovakia cede to Germany the **Sudetenland**, a territory along the German-Czech border. Hitler accused the Czechs of repressing the large German population there and asserted that the territory rightly belonged to Germany.

The September 1938 **Munich Conference** was called to address the situation; ironically, Czechoslovakia was not present. After several rounds of negotiation, and despite their own treaties with Czechoslovakia, Britain and France agreed to give in to Hitler's demand, as long as he agreed not to seize any further European territory. Hitler did sign an agreement to that effect, promising no further invasions.

After taking the Sudetenland, however, Hitler ignored the agreement and proceeded to occupy most of western Czechoslovakia, along with several other territories in eastern Europe. Britain and France again took no action. This policy of **appeasement** of Hitler's demands, which was advocated primarily by British prime minister **Neville Chamberlain**, has been much criticized as paving the road to World War II.

THE CONSEQUENCES OF APPEASEMENT

The decisions made by the Allied nations leading up to World War II, as well as those of the first six months or so after the war began, have dumbfounded historians ever since. The appeasement of Hitler, in particular, has been so often held up as an example of how *not* to deal with a rising dictator that it has become a stereotype.

However, although it may be obvious in hindsight that Hitler should not have been appeased, the actions of Prime Minister Chamberlain must be considered within the context of the time. Europe was still recovering from World War I: many of the countries of Europe were adjusting to new parliamentary governments, and the newly created **League of Nations** was a new force in international affairs. Few European leaders understood the full scope of Hitler's intentions, and a decision to go to war would have been hugely unpopular in countries, such as Britain and France, that had been so devastated in World War I. Indeed, many sincerely believed that the very concept of war had become obsolete.

THE GERMAN-SOVIET NONAGGRESSION PACT

Several months after Germany's annexation of the Sudetenland, on August 23, 1939, a fateful meeting occurred in Moscow between German foreign minister **Joachim von Ribbentrop** and Soviet foreign minister **Vyacheslav Molotov**. Afterward, they announced publicly that Germany and the USSR had signed the **German-Soviet Nonaggression Pact** to prevent hostilities between the two countries.

However, the ministers kept secret the fact that, in addition to agreeing not to attack each other, Germany and the USSR had also agreed to overrun the countries that lay between them. Specifically, they agreed that Germany and the USSR would each take over one half of Poland, with a further provision that the USSR would take over Lithuania, Latvia, and Estonia without German interference.

THE GERMAN INVASION OF POLAND

Germany's invasion of **Poland** came quickly and with overwhelming force. The attack began on September 1, 1939, with heavy air strikes followed by a rapidly advancing ground invasion. Hitler referred to the strategy as **blitzkrieg**, or "lightning war." The object of the blitzkrieg strategy was to shock the opponent so severely that there would be little resistance, allowing the country to be overrun quickly, with minimal German losses.

The primary obstacle to the German invasion force proved to be the Polish capital of **Warsaw**, which did not surrender until September 27, after a prolonged siege. By this time, all of western Poland was firmly under German control.

ATROCITIES AGAINST THE POLISH PEOPLE

Although Germany's invasion of Poland is often cited as the definitive example of the blitzkrieg tactic, not all historians share this view. Rather than rush straight to Warsaw and topple the government, Germany's forces moved relatively slowly, focusing much of their energy on targets that were neither military nor political in nature. They sought not just to destroy the Polish government but also to obliterate the Polish people. In the first days and weeks of the war, both Jewish and non-Jewish civilians were killed regardless of whether they resisted. Villages and towns were burned, and fleeing survivors were ruthlessly chased down and shot.

It was in this invasion that the real nature of Hitler's plan began to reveal itself. Although the regular German army, the **Wehrmacht**, defeated the Polish military within days of the initial invasion, a more sinister set of squadrons followed—the **Totenkopf**, or "Death's Head," part of the soon-to-be-infamous **S.S.** These squadrons immediately began rounding up and killing Polish civilians. Larger groups of **Jews** were singled out and herded into the central **Warsaw ghetto** where they were slowly starved for the next two years. Smaller groups encountered along the way were shot on the spot. Although Jews were particularly singled out, the non-Jewish Polish peasantry was treated little better. Though these atrocities would pale in comparison with what was to come, the initial weeks of Hitler's invasion were a gruesome demonstration of the German war machine's capabilities and intentions.

THE SOVIET INVASION OF POLAND

Just two weeks after the German invasion began, Soviet troops invaded Poland from the east, on September 17, 1939. It took them only two days to push far enough to meet German troops advancing from the west. By this time, Germany had already taken most of Poland except for Warsaw, which was under siege. Upon meeting the Russian troops, the Germans handed over large numbers of prisoners and promptly pulled back to the line agreed upon in the German-Soviet Nonaggression Pact. Retreating Polish armies, unaware that the USSR was part of Germany's occupation plan, fled directly into Russian hands.

ALLIED DECLARATIONS OF WAR AND THE "SITZKRIEG"

Britain and **France**—which were soon labeled the **Allied Powers,** just as they had been in World War I—both declared war on Germany on September 3, 1939, just two days after Germany began its invasion of Poland. However, aside from basic defensive preparations, neither country took significant action for several months. Rather, Britain initiated a propaganda effort against Hitler by using its bombers to drop millions of anti-Nazi leaflets over Germany. Among the British public, this effort soon came to be known as the **"confetti war."**

Germany likewise took little action after the invasion of Poland was complete, aside from several small naval attacks on Allied shipping vessels. This period of relative calm has been sarcastically labeled the **"Sitzkrieg,"** or sitting war—a play on *blitzkrieg.* Rather than make an offensive move of their own, the Allies waited for the expected German attack on **Belgium** and **France.** It would not come for many months, until the late spring of 1940.

THE RUSSO-FINNISH WAR

The one active hot spot during this "Sitzkrieg" was **Finland,** which the USSR invaded on November 30, 1939, with the goal of seizing the eastern Finnish territory of Karelia. Though vastly outnumbered and outgunned, the Finns fought back with determination and innovation, even employing troops on bicycles and skis. The invasion, which was expected to end quickly, instead lasted until March 13, 1940, when Finland finally capitulated, ceding Karelia to the Soviet

Union, along with the major port of Viipuri (present-day Vyborg). Although Finland lost territory, the victory cost the USSR more than 200,000 lives, more than twice the number that it cost the Finns.

Denmark and Norway

After months of inaction, the first sign that Hitler was again on the move came in early April 1940. On April 9, German troops simultaneously took Copenhagen, the capital of **Denmark**, and landed on the coast of **Norway**. Denmark gave in almost immediately. In Norway, although the capital at Oslo was quickly taken and a puppet government set up, a strong resistance movement supported by Britain and France continued to fight the Germans for two months. The combat was generally limited to the less densely populated areas in the north of the country.

SUMMARY & ANALYSIS

THE INVASION OF FRANCE

EVENTS

May 10, 1940	Germany begins invasions of Belgium, the Netherlands, and France
May 13	French and British troops move into Belgium but are trapped between German armies
May 14	Luftwaffe bombs central Rotterdam; Netherlands surrenders to Germany
May 27	British troops begin mass evacuation from Dunkirk
June 3	Luftwaffe initiates air raids on Paris
June 12	German forces penetrate France's final lines of defense
June 22	France signs armistice with Germany
June 23	Hitler visits Paris

THE WESTERN FRONT

After months of nervous speculation, Germany brought war to western Europe on May 10, 1940, with the primary goal of conquering **France**. German bombers hit air bases in France, **Luxembourg**, **Belgium**, and the **Netherlands**, destroying large numbers of Allied planes on the ground and crippling Allied air defenses. Elite squads of German paratroopers were dropped onto fortified Allied points along the front, neutralizing a key element of France's defense strategy.

On the ground, German forces advanced in two directions: one through the Netherlands and northern Belgium (where Britain and France had expected) and the other, larger force to the south, through Luxembourg and into the **Ardennes Forest** on a path that led directly into the French heartland. Unaware of the German advance to the south, Britain and France sent the bulk of their troops to Belgium.

THE FALL OF THE NETHERLANDS

During the first days of the attack, the Germans made slower progress toward Brussels and The Hague than expected, as the Dutch forces fought back formidably. In response, on May 14, the German air force, the **Luftwaffe**, unleashed a massive bombing attack on central **Rotterdam**, even while surrender negotiations with the Netherlands were under way. Although efforts were made to call off the attack at the last minute, only some of the German pilots got the message, so part of the attack was carried out. Over 800 civilians were killed, and the Netherlands surrendered that day.

BELGIUM

The British and French plan to defend **Belgium** was to make a stand at a line of forts between the cities of Antwerp and Liege. Unaware that these forts had already been captured by German paratrooper units on the first night of the invasion, the British and French armies found themselves under assault on May 13. At the same time, the second, unexpected German offensive to the south emerged from the Ardennes Forest. Over the next few days, the main Allied armies were trapped between the two German forces, able neither to protect Paris nor to stop the Germans from advancing to the English Channel. Then, when the German troops to the south moved between the French and British forces, the Allies were divided and thus weakened further still. The Allied defense of Belgium was unequivocally a disaster.

THE EVACUATION FROM DUNKIRK

While the main French army was trapped between the two German armies, the **British Expeditionary Force (BEF)** was being pushed to the coast near the French port of **Dunkirk**. With the BEF cornered with its back to the sea, and with little hope of reuniting with French forces, the British government decided that the BEF had to be evacuated. The evacuation, called **Operation Dynamo**, began on May 27, 1940. It took a full week to accomplish, using more than 800 civilian and military sea vessels. In all, more than 300,000 men were brought back across the English Channel to British soil. The feat was heroic—it was done under nearly constant bombardment from the Luftwaffe—but it left France completely on its own.

THE FALL OF FRANCE

With the British out of the way, the Germans began their final push against France. By June 12, German tanks had broken through the main fronts along the **Somme River** and the fortified **Maginot Line**, moving ever closer to their goal, **Paris**. During this time, the British vigorously encouraged France to resist at all costs. The new British prime minister, **Winston Churchill**, even flew to Paris himself to offer his personal encouragement. At the same time, though, the British government denied French requests for military assistance, wanting to conserve strength for Britain's own defense in the near future.

By this time, the size of the French army had been reduced by roughly half, and French leaders became resigned to an inevitable surrender. On June 22, 1940, France signed an **armistice** with Germany. Hitler insisted that it be done in the same railway car in which

Germany had surrendered to France in 1918, at the end of World War I. On June 23, Hitler flew to Paris for a brief sightseeing tour of the occupied city, during which a widely published photo was taken of Hitler standing against the backdrop of the Eiffel Tower.

REASONS FOR FRANCE'S DEFEAT

Although many have attributed Germany's rapid conquest of France to simple weakness of France's armed forces, this conclusion is incorrect. France's military at the time was actually larger and more technologically advanced than Germany's. In fact, before the invasion, a number of senior German military leaders felt strongly that Germany was unprepared to take on France militarily. During the invasion, Hitler himself was highly apprehensive and expressed disbelief at his own victories.

Rather, France fell primarily due to mistaken assumptions about how the attack would be carried out. Germany's advance through the Ardennes Forest was not anticipated, and even when French intelligence received word of it, they took little action because they did not believe that German tanks could make their way through a dense forest. Thus, the core of the French forces, reinforced by the British, was sent into Belgium, where the main attack was incorrectly expected to take place.

SUMMARY & ANALYSIS

The Battle of Britain

SUMMARY & ANALYSIS

Events

July 3, 1940	British initiate Operation Catapult to neutralize French navy
July 10	First German bombers attack over English Channel
July 19	Hitler urges Britain to make peace
August 13	Eagle Day; more than 1,400 German planes attack southern England
September 7	Beginning of "London Blitz"
September 17	Hitler indefinitely postpones plans for ground invasion of England

Key People

Winston Churchill	British prime minister who took office in May 1940; rallied British people and military during Battle of Britain

Fear in Britain

After France fell, the British government was certain that Germany's next move would be against the United Kingdom. These fears were confirmed when British intelligence intercepted coded German radio transmissions that made it clear that an invasion of Britain was imminent. Preparations in Britain had long been under way, and aircraft, guns, and ammunition were arriving by ship from the United States on a regular basis, despite the constant threat of attack by German submarines. The British would rely upon air and naval power as their primary defense, as they knew that they would quickly lose the war if German troops set foot on British soil in large numbers.

Operation Catapult

As Britain braced itself, one of its immediate goals was to prevent the **French navy** from falling into German hands. As a result, **Operation Catapult** was put into action on July 3, 1940. A British naval force based in Gibraltar was ordered to **Mers-el-Kebir**, Algeria, where much of the remaining French navy had fled. The British offered the French crews a choice: they could sail immediately for Britain and join in the fight against Germany, hand their ships over to the British, allow the British to move the ships somewhere safe in the West Indies, or scuttle their fleet. The French crews refused all four options, leaving the British little choice but to fire upon their allies, destroying the ships and killing over 1,200 French sailors. French ships at several other locations, however, were seized without incident.

THE CHANNEL BATTLE

The German code name for its plan to conquer the United Kingdom was **Operation Sea Lion**. The operation began tentatively, as a series of probing bomber attacks against British ships in the English Channel and ports in southern England in early July 1940. In fact, Hitler was still debating whether to invade Britain or Russia first.

The first German bomber attack over the Channel came on July 10, 1940. Yet even as late as July 19, Hitler made a last-minute speech advocating peace with Britain, presumably trying to buy time. Britain ignored the appeal. Skirmishes over the Channel and coastal southern England continued into August, but the Royal Air Force only rarely came out to defend the ships in the channel, preferring to hold off until the German planes got closer to the mainland, nearer to the limit of their range. As a result, British shipping in the Channel suffered heavy damage, but the RAF was able to conserve pilots and planes for the coming battle.

EAGLE DAY

In early August 1940, Hitler decided to begin massive bombing raids on air bases and military command posts in southern England, hoping to break Britain's will. Germany would withhold any attempt at a ground invasion, however, until it was clear that air superiority could be gained over England. On August 13, which the German high command labeled **"Eagle Day,"** Germany sent more than 1,400 bombers and fighters across the English Channel. The Germans brought down only thirteen British fighters that day but lost more than three times as many of their own aircraft.

Over the next several days, the Germans continued to suffer comparatively heavy losses. While this gave British pilots a certain sense of optimism, the sheer numbers of planes the Germans sent meant that many bombers were still reaching their targets. Nevertheless, even after three weeks of incessant attacks, the RAF was still very much intact.

THE LONDON BLITZ

In early September 1940, Hitler directed the Luftwaffe to shift its focus to the major British cities, including **London**. The attacks began on September 7 and continued into May of the following year. At times, they continued day and night for weeks at a time without letup. Tens of thousands of Londoners lost their lives during this time, along with thousands of residents of other British cities. In the meantime, however, British bombers were also conducting nightly air raids on central **Berlin**.

Although this **London Blitz** continued, Hitler decided on September 17, 1940, to put his plan for an invasion of Britain on hold indefinitely. It was clear that air superiority over England would be difficult to attain. Instead, Hitler turned his attention to Russia.

THE FIRST TURNING POINT

The **Battle of Britain** marked the first turning point in the war, as it was the first time that German forces failed to achieve a major goal. The Royal Air Force's strong and effective resistance caused Hitler to abandon the idea of invading Britain and to turn his attention to Russia. Although the Blitz continued to terrorize London and other cities for months to come, Britain no longer faced the threat of a ground invasion. It demonstrated to the world that with enough stubborn resistance, Hitler could be forced back.

THE IMPORTANCE OF AIR POWER

The Battle of Britain was also the first time in history when **air power** alone decided the outcome of a major battle. Hitler knew that there was no way he could invade Britain on the ground without first gaining air superiority. Churchill and the British military leadership also knew that stopping the Luftwaffe would be the key to their survival. The German air attacks against Britain were massive, but their initial intensity could not be maintained if the Germans were consistently losing twice as many aircraft as the British. Indeed, by the battle's end, Germany had lost 1,700 planes to 900 British planes.

The value of the new technology of **radar** was also effectively demonstrated for the first time. The British had built a net of radar stations along their coastline prior to the battle, and this system proved invaluable, as British controllers could see the enemy coming and scramble fighters in the right place at the right time. Radar also prevented the loss of large numbers of aircraft on the ground, as happened during the initial days of the invasion of France. Although the Germans made an effort to bomb radar stations early on, by mid-August they gave up this strategy, believing it ineffective. It was a major mistake.

Moreover, British pilots had a considerable advantage in fighting over their own turf. Whereas German pilots had limited time over their target areas before having to return home to refuel, British pilots could stay in the air longer and even return to base, refuel, and then resume the fight. Thus, the mere act of engaging the German planes, forcing them to expend fuel by diverting them from their course, meant that fewer bombs would reach intended targets. For both Britain and Germany, this air combat was a new kind of warfare, and each side's strategies were experimental in nature.

SUMMARY & ANALYSIS

ITALY AND THE MEDITERRANEAN

EVENTS

June 10, 1940	Italy declares war on Britain
June 11	Italian planes attack Malta British skirmish in African desert
September 13	Italy launches failed invasion of Egypt
October 28	Italy begins invasion of Greece
November	Greek resistance forces Italians into retreat
April 6, 1941	Germany attacks Yugoslavia
April 17	Yugoslavia surrenders
Late April	British forces retreat from Greece
May 20	German forces attack British troops on Crete
May	British forces retreat from Crete

KEY PEOPLE

Benito Mussolini	Italian Fascist prime minister whose territorial ambitions drew Italy into the war in June 1940
Erwin Rommel	German field marshal and tank specialist; helped Italian forces in Egypt; was also involved in later North African campaigns

ITALY'S ENTRANCE

On June 10, 1940, **Italy** declared war on France and Britain, largely because its Fascist prime minister, **Benito Mussolini**, had territorial and imperial ambitions of his own. At this time, Britain had already evacuated from Dunkirk, and German troops were moving steadily toward Paris—which meant it was too late for Italian forces to take a serious part in the battle. Hitler himself observed with annoyance that the Italians were in effect riding on his coattails so as to share in the spoils without having to take part in the dirty work. Nevertheless, Germany and Italy were soon allied together as the **Axis Powers**, and Italy's entrance into the war set off a chain reaction that brought war to much of the Mediterranean region.

ITALIAN CONQUESTS IN AFRICA

Following its war declaration, Italy made its first moves in **North Africa** and other regions of the southern Mediterranean. On June 11, 1940, the Italian air force attacked Malta, while, on the same day, British planes carried out a small bombing raid on the Italian colony of Eritrea (in Africa) as well as on the Italian cities of Genoa and Turin. Skirmishes continued in Africa throughout the summer, but the war there did not begin in earnest until August 3, when Italian forces invaded British **Somaliland**. This attack marked the opening of the **East Africa campaign** and was a total defeat for Britain, which was forced to abandon the area within days.

A second Italian offensive into British-occupied **Egypt** on September 13 was a catastrophic failure. Although heavily outnumbered, the British defenders decimated the Italian forces, taking large numbers of prisoners and advancing well into Italian-held territory. This Italian defeat prompted Germany to get involved by sending its best tank divisions under the command of Field Marshal **Erwin Rommel**, Germany's most celebrated commander of mechanized forces.

GREECE

The Italian invasion of **Greece** began on October 28, 1940, using forces based in Albania. Mussolini began the attack without consulting or even informing Hitler, who was incensed upon hearing the news. Greece, a country of difficult, mountainous terrain, also had a respectable army that fought the Italians doggedly. In November, Greek forces broke through the Italian line and over the next few months were able gradually to push the invaders back to the Albanian border. It was not long before Britain began providing air support in Greece's defense. As in Egypt, Mussolini had bitten off more than his military could chew. Germany, however, bided its time and allowed the Italians to flounder.

GERMANY'S INTERVENTION

By March 1941, the situation for the Italians had deteriorated so badly that Hitler was finally forced to step in. This decision raised a new problem, however, in that neutral **Yugoslavia** refused to grant German forces permission to cross its territory. Therefore, on April 6, Germany invaded Yugoslavia using its standard blitzkrieg method. Yugoslavia surrendered on April 17, and the German forces quickly moved onward to Greece.

By this time, Britain had forces on the ground in Greece to help the fight against the Germans. The British help was not enough, however, and by the end of April, all British forces had evacuated Greece, and the country fell totally under German control. One more battle broke out when the Luftwaffe struck the British garrison on the island of **Crete** on May 20. Heavy fighting followed, but by the end of the month, the British again had to evacuate.

ITALY'S EFFECT ON THE WAR

Italy's two early campaigns—North Africa and Greece—were similar in that they both were marked by early success but later became quagmires. In both cases, Germany had to intervene and, as a result, committed forces that were badly needed elsewhere. However, whereas Greece was a relatively short campaign, lasting only a few months, the war in the deserts of North Africa would go on for years. The desert war would become one of the major campaigns of World War II, involving large numbers of forces and dramatic battles. The Italian entrance into the war thus greatly expanded its geographical scope and had significant influence on Germany's decision making.

SUMMARY & ANALYSIS

THE INVASION OF RUSSIA

EVENTS

June 22, 1941	Germany begins invasion of USSR
July 1	Germany has Riga, Dvinsk, Minsk, and Lvov under control
July 3	Stalin orders scorched-earth policy
September	Hitler shifts priority of attack to southern Russia
September 8	Germans begin siege of Leningrad
September 19	Kiev falls to German forces
October	Thousands of russian civilians dig trenches around Moscow
November 27	German advance on Moscow is halted
December 8	Hitler orders all forces in USSR to shift from offensive to defensive operations
July 27, 1942	German troops cross Don River
August 23	German troops reach Volga River; Luftwaffe bombs Stalingrad
November 19–20	USSR launches two offensives against Germans
December 12	Germany launches Operation Winter Storm
February 2, 1943	German Sixth Army surrenders

KEY PEOPLE

Joseph Stalin	Soviet premier; ordered scorched-earth policy to halt German advances in USSR
Friedrich Paulus	German field marshal; defied Hitler's orders and surrendered to Soviets at Stalingrad

OPERATION BARBAROSSA

The initial German invasion of the **Soviet Union** was known as **Operation Barbarossa**. It began on June 22, 1941, after months of delay and years of planning. The general goals were to gain more land for Germany, control the oil fields of Azerbaijan, and exterminate Bolshevism—the radical Communism that Vladimir Lenin had installed in Russia during the Russian Revolution. Moreover, Hitler wanted to exterminate the "racially inferior" Russian people from Leningrad, Moscow, and the rest of the western USSR while pushing the rest of the population eastward beyond the Ural Mountains.

Despite the fact that the USSR was far larger than Germany both geographically and militarily, Hitler believed that the country would collapse quickly, after a brief show of German force. The German advance was organized into three main thrusts: one through the Baltic region, toward Leningrad; one through central Russia, toward Moscow; and one to the south, toward Kiev and the Black Sea coast. This resulted in a front line nearly 1,000 miles long, which necessitated a gargantuan Axis force of approximately 4 million soldiers, 3 million of whom were German. Although Hitler hoped to complete the operation by the onset of winter in late 1941, Germany's conflict with the Soviet Union would continue for most of the war.

THE GERMAN AIR ATTACK

Much like Hitler's previous invasions, the attack on the USSR began by air and concentrated on Russian frontline airbases. The Soviet Union had a substantially larger, though less modern, air force than Germany, and destroying it was crucial to Germany's success. The German attack began in the predawn hours of June 22 and continued without letup nearly all day. Though estimates vary significantly, the USSR lost between 1,200 and 2,000 aircraft—approximately one quarter of its entire air force—the first day. Most of these aircraft were destroyed on the ground, parked at their airbases. Over the next week, the Soviets lost an additional 2,000 to 3,000 in battle. The setback was devastating and would take the USSR a long time to overcome.

THE GERMAN ADVANCE

The German attack caught the Soviet military completely off guard, and its forces were not positioned to respond effectively to the attacks. In its confusion, the Soviet high command issued contradictory orders, and Soviet premier **Joseph Stalin** hesitated before ordering decisive action. In the meantime, German forces advanced quickly across the Russian countryside. In little more than a week, by July 1, the Germans had pushed 200 to 300 miles into Russia and captured the major cities of Riga and Dvinsk in the north, Minsk in the central region, and Lvov in the south.

REASONS FOR THE USSR's VULNERABILITY

Even prior to the invasion, Stalin had made several decisions that severely weakened his country's ability to respond to the German threat. First, during his infamous **purges** of the 1930s, Stalin had most of the Soviet military leadership murdered or sent to labor camps in Siberia. Because this group included many seasoned officers, Russia's military leadership in 1941 was much less experienced than it had been only five or six years before. Second, Stalin had resisted early recommendations by his military leaders to mobilize forces along the western border or to take steps to protect air bases from attack. Stalin's motives in this matter have never been clear.

SUMMARY & ANALYSIS

THE RUSSIAN RESPONSE

Despite these setbacks, the USSR still put up a formidable fight. Unlike most of the enemy forces that the Germans had encountered in western Europe, the Soviet troops tended either to retreat or fight to the last man—not surrender. Within days of the invasion, the Soviets organized small partisan groups and "destruction battalions" and sent them behind enemy lines to interfere with German efforts in numerous ways.

On July 3, Stalin ordered the Soviet army to implement a **scorched-earth policy** and either destroy or remove all useful supplies or facilities before retreating so that these resources would not fall into German hands. The Russians thus destroyed roads and bridges, burned fields of crops, and demolished or emptied many factories. Some major factories were even disassembled and moved eastward out of danger. The scorched-earth policy was effective and hindered the advancing German armies.

THE WESTERN RESPONSE

Although Britain and the United States were wary of Stalin and Russian Communism in general, the idea that the entire USSR might fall to the Germans was unacceptable. Within days of the invasion, Britain began providing Stalin with intelligence information gleaned directly from secret German transmissions that Allied code breakers had cracked and continued to read on a daily basis. In early July, the British also intensified their bombing of Berlin and other major German cities in an effort to force Hitler to recall some of the Luftwaffe forces back to Germany.

By late July, the first allied shipments of military supplies began reaching ports in the northern USSR. These shipments from Britain and the United States continued to grow significantly and included large numbers of aircraft and tanks, as well as food and medical supplies. From August 10–14, Churchill and Roosevelt met onboard a ship off Newfoundland and together laid out an extensive plan for providing large-scale assistance to the USSR.

KIEV AND LENINGRAD

By early September 1941, German forces had moved deep into European Russia, within easy reach of the major cities of **Kiev** and **Leningrad**. On September 10, Hitler decided to concentrate on the invasion of southern Russia and the Ukraine, hoping to gain access to the region's economic resources, which included the wheat fields of the Ukraine, the citrus farms of the Black Sea coast, and the oil fields of the Caucasus.

On September 12, Hitler ordered the northern forces to cease their advance on Leningrad. Rather than enter the city, they were ordered to hold their current position, encircle the city, and slowly starve it to death. This strategy would allow several German tank divisions in the Leningrad area to be diverted for use in the south. Thus began the famous 900-day **siege of Leningrad**.

With more German troops available for in the south, the Ukraine collapsed quickly. After the Germans captured nearly half a million Soviet troops outside Kiev, the Ukrainian capital fell on September 19.

THE RUSSIAN WINTER

Hitler originally planned for the campaign against the Soviet Union to take six weeks. Although the Germans did initially make very fast progress, the farther into the USSR they traveled, the more things slowed down. In the meantime, summer turned to autumn, bringing a constant, miserable mix of rain and snow. During October, the roads turned to mud, effectively halting the German advance. By November, snow covered the ground, and temperatures were so cold that they interfered with the operation of equipment. German soldiers, still in summer uniforms, succumbed to frostbite and hypothermia in large numbers. Hitler nonetheless ordered them to continue.

The winter gave the Soviet armies a new advantage, as they were far better prepared to fight under such conditions. Moreover, reinforcements from the Russian Far East arrived in large numbers, while the tanks and planes sent from Britain and the United States were finally entering combat. German intelligence was unaware of these reinforcements, leaving the German troops in for a nasty surprise.

MOSCOW

As the Germans approached **Moscow**, they encountered row after row after row of trenches and ditches reinforced by barbed wire. Since late October, thousands of Russian civilians had dug more than 5,000 miles of trenches by hand all the way around the city. On November 27, 1941, these trenches finally brought the German advance on Moscow to a halt, less than twenty miles from the Kremlin.

Overwhelmed by a strong Russian defense, frigid temperatures, and constant harassment by Russian partisans behind the lines, the Germans became mired. In just three weeks, they lost 85,000 men—

the same number that they had lost over the entire Barbarossa campaign up to that point. During the first week of December, the Germans slowly began losing ground, and the Soviets managed to push them back for several miles. Although the Germans still did not retreat, on December 8, 1941, a directive issued from Hitler himself instructed all German troops in Russia to shift from offensive operations to defensive.

COSTS OF THE INVASION FOR GERMANY

Most historians would agree that Hitler's decision to invade the USSR was one of the main reasons that Germany lost the war. German forces were tied up in this conflict for years. It drained Germany's resources, hurt morale, and diverted its military presence from western Europe, ultimately making it possible for British and American forces to invade France in 1944.

Germany's failure in Russia was the result of several gross miscalculations. Hitler underestimated how long the operation would take, how hard the Russians would fight, how successful Russian partisan actions would be, and how quickly and effectively the Allies would come to the Soviet Union's aid. Hitler also failed to comprehend how difficult it would be to maintain control of such a huge territory or how poorly prepared the German military was for fighting in Russia's climate.

DEVASTATION IN THE USSR

The scope of the devastation that occurred in the Soviet Union during World War II is poorly appreciated in the West and indeed hard even to fathom. Germany carried out the invasion with a brutality rarely seen in human history. Twenty million people died in Russia at the hands of the invaders—a total that includes soldiers fighting on the front, Jews who were singled out and murdered in Russian towns, local government officials, and millions of ordinary Russian citizens who were killed with the same calculating methodology. One of Hitler's specific goals for the invasion was to substantially reduce the overall population of the western Soviet Union to make more room for the Germans whom he intended to move there. The scale of the killing was so great that even some members of the German death squads became overwhelmed by the grotesqueness of their orders.

THE PUSH FOR STALINGRAD

After the stalemate near Moscow over the winter of 1941–1942, Germany shifted the focus of its invasion force to the south, where it had already captured most of the Ukraine, and sent most of its troops across the southern Russian steppes. On July 27, 1942, these forces crossed the Don River and made for the industrial center of **Stalingrad**. Yet another prong of the German offensive was heading even farther south, into the region of the Caucasus Mountains. In the meantime, resistance by Soviet **partisans** behind the German lines continued with increasing success.

THE VOLGA RIVER

The Germans reached the **Volga River** on August 23, 1942, to the north of Stalingrad, and made ready for an all-out assault on the city. On the same day, hundreds of German bombers struck Stalingrad with enough ordinance to set off a firestorm, and the Volga itself caught fire after the burning contents of local oil reserves spilled into the river. Approximately 40,000 residents of Stalingrad died during the initial assault. Encouraged by the early success, German commanders believed that Stalingrad would be a quick victory. As it turned out, it would become one of the deadliest single battles in history and would last for six months.

URBAN BATTLE

Within days, the German army entered Stalingrad, where Soviet forces were waiting. Both Stalin and Hitler had forbidden their troops from retreating under any circumstances. For months, the fighting moved street by street, block by block, and the city was gutted to a skeleton of its former self as the Germans launched repeated air raids involving up to 1,000 planes at a time. On the ground, troops from both sides took cover in bombed-out buildings, tanks roamed awkwardly through rubble-strewn streets, and Russian and German snipers hid in the ruins and tried to pick off enemy soldiers.

Stalin ordered thousands of additional Soviet troops from other regions to be amassed to the north of Stalingrad and sent the majority of Russia's military aircraft to the city's defense. Meanwhile, the Germans surrounded the city from the west, trapping the Russian defenders inside the city. The Germans failed to gain control of the Volga River, however, and the Russians were able to send in food and supplies via that route.

ANOTHER RUSSIAN WINTER

As the autumn of 1942 waned, the German army faced its second winter in Russia. The Germans attempted to bring in supplies for the winter, but powerful Soviet air defenses combined with vicious snowstorms proved too much of an obstacle. On November 19–20, the Russians launched two new offensive actions from the north and the south, which eventually surrounded the entire German Sixth Army. The German commander on the scene, Field Marshal **Friedrich Paulus**, requested permission to break free and retreat to the Don River. Hitler refused and ordered him to fight on, even as food and supplies were running out.

On December 12, Germany launched **Operation Winter Storm** in an attempt to rescue the trapped army, but the action failed. The Sixth Army struggled on as its soldiers slowly starved. At the end of January 1943, Paulus decided to defy Hitler's orders and surrender. By February 2, all remaining German forces at Stalingrad had given up to the Soviets.

COSTS OF THE BATTLE OF STALINGRAD

Historians estimate that approximately 2 million people died in the Battle of Stalingrad, more than 800,000 on the German side and 1.1 million on the Soviet side. After the battle, little of the city itself remained, and it would not be reconstructed fully for decades. Despite the catastrophic losses, the Soviet victory stood as solid proof to the world that the Third Reich was not invincible.

JAPAN AND PEARL HARBOR

EVENTS

1937	Japan goes to war with China
July 1939	Roosevelt announces that Treaty of Commerce and Navigation will not be renewed
July 2, 1940	U.S. Congress passes Export Control Act
August	Japan declares greater East Asia co-prosperity sphere
September 27	Japan signs Tripartite Pact with Germany and Italy
January 1941	Yamamoto prepares plan for attack on Pearl Harbor
July	Japanese troops occupy Indochina
October	Hirohito gives general approval for Pearl Harbor attack
November 8	Hirohito approves formal battle plan for attack in December
November 26	Japanese attack fleet sets sail from Japan
December 7	Japan launches surprise attack on Pearl Harbor
December 8	United States and Britain declare war on Japan
December 11	Germany declares war on United States

KEY PEOPLE

Franklin D. Roosevelt	32nd U.S. president; implemented economic penalties that angered Japan; requested war declaration after Japanese attacked Pearl Harbor in December 1941
Yamamoto Isoroku	Japanese admiral who planned surprise attack at Pearl Harbor
Hirohito	Japanese emperor; approved Pearl Harbor attack plan
Richmond K. Turner	U.S. Navy admiral; warned that navy be put on high alert status and security increased at Pearl Harbor, but recommendations were implemented only partly

TENSIONS IN THE PACIFIC

In the years prior to the outbreak of World War II in Europe, tensions were also escalating in the Pacific region. **Japan**, which had been at war with **China** since 1937, had declared openly its intent to take over as much of eastern Asia as it could. It also had serious ambitions toward taking territory in the Soviet Union. If Germany, which the Japanese government saw as a potential ally, would attack Russia from the west, Japanese military leaders felt that they stood a good chance of seizing Soviet-controlled territory in the east. The signing of the German-Soviet Nonaggression Pact in 1939 therefore caused a huge scandal in Japan, as it directly undermined Japan's plans.

JAPAN AND THE UNITED STATES

In the meantime, the **United States** was becoming more and more of a problem for Japan. Throughout the 1930s, the United States and many European nations, suffering from the **Great Depression**, enacted high protective tariffs. These tariffs greatly curbed Japanese exports and heightened the effects of their own economic depression. The poor economic conditions caused strong anti-Western sentiment in Japan and were a strong factor in forcing the Japanese invasion of China.

In July 1939, President **Franklin D. Roosevelt** decided not to renew the 1911 U.S.-Japan **Treaty of Commerce and Navigation**, which was due to expire in January 1940. Then, on July 2, 1940, the U.S. Congress passed the **Export Control Act**. Together, these two actions effectively eliminated Japan's primary source of oil, scrap metal, and other material resources needed for war.

These developments dealt not only a severe economic blow to Japan but also a humiliating slap in the face to Japan's leaders, who felt that the United States had no right to pass judgment on them or to interfere in their affairs. Although Japan was still smarting from the German-Soviet Nonaggression Pact, the United States' actions were enough to overcome this resentment, and on September 27, 1940, Japan signed the **Tripartite Pact** with Germany and Italy. The pact made the three nations official allies.

THE UNITED STATES PREPARES FOR WAR

Although the United States remained officially neutral during the first two years of World War II, the Roosevelt administration was far from indifferent or oblivious to the conflict. The United States provided material support first to Britain and later to the Soviet Union, secretly at first but then with increasing openness over time. Chief among these measures was the March 1941 **Lend-Lease Act**, which empowered Roosevelt to give aid to the Allies in exchange for whatever kind of compensation or benefit the president deemed acceptable. The American people also paid close attention to the events developing in the Pacific and, by mid-1941, considered war with both Japan and Germany to be likely possibilities.

U.S. intelligence services had direct access to Japanese coded transmissions, so U.S. officials were well aware that the Japanese were planning something against them—they just did not know precisely what. One man in particular, Admiral **Richmond K. Turner**, strongly urged that U.S. forces be placed on a higher state of alert, as he was particularly concerned about the U.S. Navy base at **Pearl Harbor**, Hawaii. During previous U.S. war games and exercises, Pearl Harbor had proven highly vulnerable to surprise attacks. Although Turner's advice was considered, only some of his recommendations were implemented.

INDOCHINA

Indochina was a French-administered colony in Southeast Asia comprising the present-day nations Vietnam, Laos, and Cambodia. On July 20, 1941, Japanese troops entered the region and quickly occupied the entire area. Japan justified the occupation as necessary in order to deny resources to the Chinese resistance. However, Indochina also provided Japan with a convenient base for launching attacks against other countries and territories in the region, including Singapore and the Dutch East Indies. Both the United States and Britain saw this move as a threat and a clear indication of Japan's intention to continue its expansion throughout the Pacific Rim. The two countries expressed their disapproval by freezing Japanese bank accounts.

THE JAPANESE ATTACK PLAN

As early as January 1941, Admiral **Yamamoto Isoroku** developed a plan for attacking the U.S. fleet at Pearl Harbor and carried out training exercises to prepare specifically for such an attack. In October, the Japanese emperor, **Hirohito**, gave his general approval for action against the United States and, on November 8, approved the specific Pearl Harbor attack plan.

On November 25–26, the Japanese fleet set sail from Japan, unseen by U.S. spies. Even then, however, some Japanese officials disapproved of the plan, and it continued to be debated heatedly. By December 1, all discussion had ended, and Hirohito ordered the plan to proceed. Japan's goal was to make a permanent end to Western interference in its affairs by obliterating the U.S. and British military capabilities in the Pacific.

PEARL HARBOR

On the morning of December 7, 1941, a fleet of six aircraft carriers, twenty-five submarines, and nearly three dozen additional support ships was sitting 200 miles north of the Hawaiian island of **Oahu**—in the open sea, far beyond the line of sight of any U.S. forces. The first wave of Japanese planes numbered more than 180. Although U.S. radar operators saw the massive formation nearly a full hour before the attack began, they raised no alarm, because they mistook the planes for a group of U.S. bombers expected to arrive from California around the same time. This mistake happened in spite of the fact that the planes seen on the radar were coming from the wrong direction and were much more numerous than the expected bomber fleet.

The first wave arrived at the U.S. Navy base at **Pearl Harbor** at 7:55 A.M. and achieved complete surprise; only nine Japanese planes were lost. The primary targets were major U.S. warships, most of which were docked close together in neat lines. These included eight of the nine battleships in the U.S. Pacific Fleet, along with several dozen other warships. The Japanese also targeted six nearby military airfields. A second attack wave of more than 160 planes followed just over an hour later. By this time, the Americans were well alerted and managed to bring down twenty Japanese planes.

In all, the attack on Pearl Harbor killed 2,402 Americans, destroyed five battleships completely, put three more out of commission, sank or seriously damaged at least eleven other warships, and destroyed nearly more than 180 aircraft on the ground. The only good luck the U.S. Navy had was that none of its aircraft carriers were in port at the time and that the Japanese bombers failed to hit the large fuel reserves in the area.

In addition to attacking Pearl Harbor that day, Japan also attacked the U.S. territories of Guam, the Philippines, Wake Island, and Midway Island, as well as British interests in Malaya and Hong Kong.

DECLARATIONS OF WAR

The next day, December 8, Roosevelt went before both houses of the U.S. Congress to request a **declaration of war** against Japan; after a vote, the declaration was formalized just hours later. Britain declared war on Japan on the same day. Three days later, on December 11, **Germany** declared war on the United States. Thus, the United States was now at war with both Japan and Germany and able to enter fully into its alliance with Britain.

REACTION IN THE UNITED STATES

The story of the attack on Pearl Harbor has become a part of American culture. For the American population, the event was a traumatic shock, as few regular Americans knew much about the events in Japan leading up to the war or about the level of hostility that Japan bore toward the United States. Officials in the U.S. government, however, could not claim such obliviousness. Uncomfortable questions were soon raised in Congress and on the streets about why the United States had been so poorly prepared and why the U.S. intelligence services had failed to see the attack coming or raise warnings earlier.

Over the years, historical analysis has shown that there were many warning signs in the months before the attack and that some U.S. military leaders, most notably Admiral Turner, had been concerned that the Pearl Harbor base was particularly vulnerable to attack. Furthermore, the United States was able to decode and read Japanese military communications until shortly before the attack, when Japan abruptly changed its military codes. By the evening of December 6, 1941, U.S. military and government officials, including President Roosevelt, were certain that Japan was planning a major action against U.S. interests. A meeting was even scheduled for 3:00 P.M. on December 7 to discuss the matter. Unfortunately, the target of the attack was unknown, and no one at Pearl Harbor was notified to be on alert.

To this day, there is avid speculation about how much the United States could and should have done to prevent the attack, and even more speculation over how much the United States and its allies knew about Japanese plans. Britain's prime minister, **Winston Churchill**, was desperate for active U.S. participation and had long been pressing his old friend Roosevelt to enter the war. Some historians maintain that British intelligence had specific information about the Pearl Harbor attack and that Churchill deliberately kept the information to himself so that the United States would finally go to war. These claims, however, remain unconfirmed.

SUMMARY & ANALYSIS

THE NAZIS' "FINAL SOLUTION"

EVENTS

December 8, 1941	Concentration camp at Chelmno, Poland, begins gassing Jewish prisoners
January 20, 1942	Wannsee Conference held

THE BEGINNING OF THE HOLOCAUST

While the United States was becoming embroiled in the war in the Pacific, back in Europe the true intent of the Nazi armies was becoming increasingly clear. As more and more of eastern Europe fell into German hands, the territory became a sort of backyard for the Nazis, where the ugliest parts of their plan could be carried out far away from prying eyes. By late 1941, the first Jews from Germany and western Europe were gathered and transported, along with many other minorities, to **concentration camps** in Poland, Czechoslovakia, Lithuania, Latvia, Ukraine, and western Russia, where they were first used as slaves and then systematically murdered.

At this point, the notorious **gas chambers** of the later Nazi concentration camps were not yet common. Most victims were taken in groups to secluded areas where they were stripped of clothing, pushed into open pits, machine-gunned, and then quickly covered over, in many cases even before all were dead. Indeed, one of the reasons for creating the gas chambers and extermination camps was that many troops in the German **S.S.** experienced severe psychological repercussions carrying out the gruesome tasks put before them.

The German atrocities were not directed solely at Jews. Precisely the same fate awaited millions of non-Jewish Russian and eastern European civilians, as well as many Soviet prisoners of war. By December 1941, the number of Nazi murders was already in the hundreds of thousands and growing rapidly.

THE WANNSEE CONFERENCE

On January 20, 1942, a group of fifteen Nazi officials met in a villa in the Wannsee district outside Berlin in order to settle the details for resolving the so-called **"Jewish question."** The meeting was led by Reinhard Heydrich, chief of the **Gestapo** (the Nazi secret police), and included several members of the S.S. along with representatives of several German government ministries. Neither Hitler nor any heads of government ministries were present.

The topics discussed at the **Wannsee Conference** included the logistics of expelling Jews from Germany by emigration, the possibility of mandatory sterilization, and the best ways to deal with people of mixed blood. The conference devoted considerable attention to the matter of who would be legally considered a Jew; ultimately, it set different conditions for pure Jews and those of mixed blood, in turn classified by first generation and second generation. Delegates also discussed how to handle Jews who would not or could not leave the country; it was decided that these Jews would be sterilized and sent to live in all-Jewish "retirement ghettos."

The official record of the Wannsee Conference made no mention of mass killing of Jews or of extermination camps. However, the meeting did set a secret goal to remove 11 million Jews from Europe by whatever means and expressed concern that the mass emigration process already taking place was becoming expensive and more difficult to negotiate. The terms "final solution" and "absolute final solution" were used, although the specifics were not elaborated.

THE DEATH CAMPS

Nazi forces had begun the mass killing of Jews as early as 1939, when Germany first invaded Poland. These actions expanded greatly during the invasion of the USSR in 1941. By 1942, the so-called *Endlösung*, or **"final solution,"** took shape, as the murders become increasingly systematic and Hitler pressed his underlings to speed up the process. During the previous year, S.S. commanders had experimented with different methods, and gas chambers proved to be the method of choice.

Although prisoners died by the thousands from disease, overwork, or starvation in German labor camps throughout Europe, there were only seven designated **extermination camps**. Six were located in Poland, one in Belorussia. These camps existed purely for the purpose of killing, and most of the prisoners taken to them were dead within hours of arrival. A limited number of prisoners deemed fit enough to work were temporarily forced to labor in these camps, but they were underfed and overworked until they too were unfit for labor and subsequently killed.

More than 90 percent of the victims sent to these extermination camps were Jews, brought in from all over Germany and other German-controlled areas of eastern and western Europe. **Romany** (Gypsies) and **homosexuals** also lost their lives in the camps in significant numbers, as did some Soviet prisoners of war. The camps continued operation virtually unimpeded until the Allies finally liberated them near the end of the war.

TOTAL WAR IN THE PACIFIC

EVENTS

February 15, 1942	Japan captures Singapore
March 9	Japan captures Java
April 9	Japan captures the Philippines
April 18	Doolittle Raid on Tokyo
May 4–8	Battle of the Coral Sea
June 3–6	Battle of Midway

KEY PEOPLE

James Doolittle	U.S. Army colonel who led daring air raid on Japanese mainland in April 1942
Yamomoto Isoroku	Japanese admiral who orchestrated attacks on both Pearl Harbor and Midway

THE JAPANESE ONSLAUGHT

After its initial attacks on Pearl Harbor and Allied interests throughout the Pacific, the Japanese navy continued to expand its conquests over the coming months. On February 15, 1942, Japanese forces took **Singapore**, which was a very humiliating defeat for Britain. On March 9, after a series of extended sea battles, the Dutch colony of **Java** surrendered. On April 9, the U.S. territory of the **Philippines** also fell to Japan. Island colonies, territories, and nations in Southeast Asia continued to fall one after the other as Japanese forces exploded across the South China Sea and into the Bay of Bengal, threatening **Burma** and even **India**.

THE DOOLITTLE RAID

On April 18, 1942, U.S. forces launched a daring air raid to demonstrate that Japan itself was susceptible to Allied attack. Lieutenant Colonel **James Doolittle** led the ingenious campaign, which originated from the aircraft carrier USS *Hornet*. Although aircraft carriers were designed to launch fighters, not bombers, Doolittle specially prepared a squadron of sixteen B-25 bombers to fly from the *Hornet*. The bombers were stripped of all equipment and parts not absolutely necessary for the flight and loaded on board the *Hornet* with a minimum cargo of bombs.

The lightweight planes managed to take off from the *Hornet* and fly more than 800 miles to Japan, where they dropped bombs on oil reservoirs and naval facilities in Tokyo and several other cities. The planes then continued on to China to land. Low on fuel, all sixteen planes crash-landed, but two went astray into Japanese-held territory and another landed in Vladivostok, in the eastern USSR. Although the raid did minimal damage to Japan, it was a powerful psychological victory for the United States and demonstrated that the Japanese homeland was indeed vulnerable.

THE BATTLE OF THE CORAL SEA

By late spring 1942, Japan had captured most of Southeast Asia and turned its attention southward. In early May, Japanese invasion fleets were ordered to take over Tulagi in the **Solomon Islands** and Port Moresby on **New Guinea**—the location of a major Allied base and the last Allied outpost standing between the Japanese navy and **Australia**. U.S. forces in the area were alerted in advance because of intercepted Japanese radio transmissions. Two American aircraft carriers (the USS *Lexington* and USS *Yorktown*), along with several cruisers and destroyers, were dispatched to stop the attacks and protect Port Moresby. The Japanese landed at Tulagi on May 3, before American ships could arrive on the scene. The next day, planes from the *Lexington* attacked the Japanese forces on the ground at Tulagi and then turned south to join the *Yorktown* in defending Port Moresby.

The Americans and Japanese finally engaged each other on May 7 in the **Battle of the Coral Sea**. The entire battle was carried out by carrier-based aircraft, without any ships exchanging shots—the first time in history that a naval battle was waged exclusively from the air. Both sides suffered heavy losses, and the *Lexington* was sunk. While material losses were comparable for each side, the Allied forces succeeded in their central goal of protecting Port Moresby.

JAPAN'S NEW PLAN

Following the humiliation of the Doolittle Raid and the failure to take Port Moresby during the Battle of the Coral Sea, Japanese strategists knew that something had to be done to eliminate the threat from U.S. aircraft carriers. Admiral **Yamamoto Isoroku**, who had planned the Pearl Harbor attack, was again put in charge.

Yamamoto's plan involved a massive assault on the Pacific island of **Midway** and a second, smaller attack on the **Aleutian Islands** of Alaska with the intent of drawing part of the U.S. Navy away from Midway. The Japanese assembled a huge armada of more than 150 ships for the attack, including four aircraft carriers and seven battleships. As with the Battle of the Coral Sea, however, U.S. intelligence managed to decipher Japanese coded transmissions and determine where the actual attack would take place. The United States responded by sending its entire Pacific Fleet to Midway.

The Battle of Midway

After light U.S. bombing of the Japanese carriers on June 3, 1942, Japan initiated the attack early in the morning on June 4, bombing the U.S. base on Midway Island. American naval planes responded against the Japanese armada in a series of waves. Although the first American attacks were easily repulsed, a group of U.S. dive-bombers finally got through Japanese defenses and near three Japanese aircraft carriers, whose decks were loaded with freshly fueled aircraft preparing for takeoff. The American bombers managed to hit the planes on all three carriers' decks, setting off a chain of explosions that engulfed the ships in flames and set off ammunition stores in the lower decks of the giant ships. All three carriers were put out of commission and were eventually scuttled by the Japanese themselves. That afternoon, a fourth Japanese carrier was damaged beyond repair.

The **Battle of Midway** was over by the end of the day. In all, the United States lost one aircraft carrier, one destroyer, nearly 150 airplanes, and just over 300 men. The Japanese toll was far worse: four aircraft carriers, along with more than 230 airplanes and more than 2,000 men.

Japan on the Defensive

The nature of the war in the Pacific changed dramatically during the first half of 1942. Japan had begun with a strong offensive but quickly overextended itself by conquering most of Southeast Asia. Furthermore, Japan underestimated the U.S. Navy and took a risky gamble in its attack on Midway. Japan's losses at Coral Sea and Midway forced it to shift into a defensive mode. Never again would Australia or the U.S. mainland face a serious danger from Japanese attack. Although the war in the Pacific was far from over, for the rest of the World War II, Japan's struggle would remain a fight to maintain the territory it had already conquered, rather than an aggressive campaign for further expansion. Eventually, Japan would gradually lose all of these earlier gains.

THE STRENGTHENING ALLIANCE

EVENTS

January 12, 1943	Roosevelt and Churchill begin meeting at Casablanca
November 28	Churchill, Roosevelt, and Stalin begin meeting at Tehran

KEY PEOPLE

Winston Churchill	British prime minister; insisted on unconditional surrender for Germany and delayed invasion of western Europe
Franklin D. Roosevelt	32nd U.S. president; agreed to continued commitment of United States to defeat Germany in Europe
Joseph Stalin	Soviet premier; met with Churchill and Roosevelt at Tehran; pushed for early invasion of western Europe to take German pressure off the USSR

THE CASABLANCA CONFERENCE

On January 12–23, 1943, U.S. president **Franklin D. Roosevelt** and British prime minister **Winston Churchill** met at **Casablanca** in French North Africa (present-day Morocco) and decided that they would accept nothing but an **unconditional surrender** from Germany in order to end the war. They also made a number of important strategic decisions. They discussed troop distribution in the Pacific, outlined major lines of attack in the far east, and agreed upon the invasion of Sicily. Moreover, they decided to delay plans for an Allied invasion of Europe via the English Channel until the summer of 1944, due to ongoing difficulties with the preparations. Finally, in order to reduce pressure on the Soviet Union, they agreed to intensify bombing operations against Germany. Following the conference, the two leaders sent a telegram to Soviet premier **Joseph Stalin**, informing him of their decisions and reaffirming their commitment to work together with the USSR in defeating Germany.

THE TEHRAN CONFERENCE

From November 28 to December 1, 1943, Churchill, Roosevelt, and Stalin all met together for the first time, at a conference in **Tehran**, Iran. The three leaders discussed detailed plans for the Allied invasion of Europe, which Churchill and Roosevelt had decided to postpone at the Casablanca Conference earlier that year. The invasion would be code-named **Operation Overlord**. Stalin was frustrated by the delay, but Churchill and Roosevelt insisted that the extra time was needed to sufficiently degrade Germany's military strength. At the end of the meeting, Stalin committed the USSR to enter the war against Japan once Germany was defeated.

SOUTHEAST ASIA

EVENTS

March 8, 1942	Japan takes Rangoon, Burma
July	Japan occupies Guadalcanal
August 7	Allies launch offensive on Guadalcanal
November	Allies launch offensive in New Guinea
February 9, 1943	Battle of Guadalcanal ends
August 4, 1944	Allied forces take Myitkyina, Burma
October 20	Battle of Leyte begins
December 31	Battle of Leyte ends
February 19, 1945	Battle of Iwo Jima begins
February 23	U.S. Marines reach Mt. Suribachi
March 26	Iwo Jima declared secure
April 1	Battle of Okinawa begins
May 3	Allies liberate Rangoon
June 21	Battle of Okinawa ends

GUADALCANAL

After the Japanese defeat at Midway in June 1942, the war in the Pacific shifted south, as the Japanese focused on winning complete control of the **Solomon Islands**. They already had a strong foothold at the north end of the island chain, but occupying the central island, **Guadalcanal**, was crucial. When the Japanese took Guadalcanal in July 1942, the move threatened Allied shipping throughout the region, and Allied leaders were determined to respond. On August 7, the Allies launched an offensive on Guadalcanal via an amphibious landing of more than 16,000 U.S. Marines onto the island. The landing went relatively smoothly, although the Japanese naval forces sank eight Allied cruisers, two heavy carriers, and fourteen destroyers, killing more than 1,000 men.

Once on the island, the Marines found little resistance at first, since the only Japanese present were construction workers building military facilities. The Americans soon captured an airfield, which they quickly made operational, and all was quiet except for a series of Japanese air raids, which were fought off with the help of U.S. naval air support. By mid-October, however, Japan began streaming troops onto the opposite end of the island, sending wave after wave of soldiers despite terrible losses to American gunfire. The Japanese fought to the last man in virtually every engagement, regardless of the odds, which was shocking and intimidating to the U.S. troops. Attrition and limited supplies eventually resulted in unsustainable losses for the Japanese, but it was a slow process: the Battle of Guadalcanal continued until February 1943, when Japan was forced to abandon the island.

NEW GUINEA

While the Allied campaign in Guadalcanal was going on, the United States and Australia launched a joint offensive on November 16, 1942, into **New Guinea**, the control of which the Japanese and Allied forces had both been struggling over for many months. As at Guadalcanal, the Japanese displayed a tenacious will to fight for every inch of territory, regardless of the cost in human lives. Although the majority of Japanese forces were driven off the island by January 1943, the Allies were unable to remove them fully, and fighting in New Guinea continued well into 1944.

BURMA

Japan's conquests in Southeast Asia during the first half of 1942 extended as far west as **Burma**. Britain, along with its colonial armies in India, took responsibility for containing this portion of the conflict. The British campaign did not go well, however, and on March 8, 1942, the Burmese port of **Rangoon** fell to Japan. This setback was a particularly bitter loss for the Allies, as it had been a primary supply point and the site of a crucial base for the British Royal Air Force. By May, the Japanese had driven the Allies back across the Indian border. During the rest of 1942, British-Indian forces launched minor offensives into Burma, but with little success.

It was only in mid-1943, when the Allies organized a new command structure in the region—the **Southeast Asia Command**—that they made any substantial progress in driving the Japanese back. Under this new command, the British cooperated with the Chinese to advance on the Burmese border, while U.S. and British special operations forces went behind enemy lines to cut communications and create chaos in general. A major focus of the campaign was to capture the town of Myitkyina, which was a principal Japanese communications post. There was a prolonged struggle for the Myitkyina, which finally fell on August 4, 1944. Another goal was to secure the so-called **Burma Road**, which linked Burma and China but was blocked by Japanese forces. The Burma Road was reopened in January, 1945. Finally, the Allies recaptured Rangoon on May 3, 1945.

SUMMARY & ANALYSIS

THE ISLAND CAMPAIGNS

Following their success in the Solomon Islands, the Allies fought fiercely throughout 1944 and 1945 to free the many other South Pacific island groups that Japan had seized earlier in the war. Many of these islands had formerly been territories of the United States, Britain, or other Allied countries. The largest of the island groups included the Marshall Islands, the Marianas, the Philippines, and the Ryukyu Islands. The battles took place on land, on the sea, and in the air.

For Japan, it was a nearly continuous series of losses, beginning with the **Battle of the Philippine Sea** near the Mariana Islands on June 19–20, 1944. In this huge sea battle, Japan lost most of its naval air power. Three Japanese aircraft carriers were sunk and more than 300 airplanes destroyed. The ground battles in these campaigns were similar in character to those on Guadalcanal and New Guinea: the fighting involved guerilla-style warfare with very high casualty counts, especially for the Japanese. For example, in the **Battle of Leyte**, which took place in the Philippines between October 20 and December 31, 1944, the Japanese lost 49,000 soldiers out of a total of 55,000 involved in the conflict. In the same conflict, the United States lost only 3,500 troops.

One by one, the Allies liberated Japanese-controlled islands until the last obstacle between Allied forces and the Japanese mainland were the Ryukyu Islands, which included **Okinawa**. However, each battle was more intense and more costly than the previous one, which led military commanders to begin rethinking their strategy.

IWO JIMA

A small island off the Japanese coast, **Iwo Jima** served as an early warning station against Allied bombers en route to attack Japan. As the Allies closed in on Japan, Iwo Jima became an obvious target. Following a heavy bombardment of the island by aircraft and battleships, U.S. Marines began an amphibious assault on February 19, 1945. Over 20,000 Japanese troops were garrisoned on Iwo Jima, and the entire island was honeycombed with underground tunnels and bunkers, especially **Mt. Suribachi**, which overlooked the southern end of the island.

After U.S. forces came ashore, they surrounded the base of Mt. Suribachi within a single day. Ascending the mountain was another matter entirely, as the Japanese fought from their hidden tunnels and small bunkers on the steep, ash-covered slopes. After a brutal, four-day struggle, U.S. forces reached the peak of Mt. Suribachi on February 23, where an Associated Press photographer took a now world-famous photograph of a group of Marines raising the American flag. Although taking the mountain was a victory in itself, it would be more than a month before U.S. forces secured the entire island. Approximately 20,000 Japanese soldiers—nearly all the forces on the island—were killed. The American death toll was 7,000.

OKINAWA

The **Battle of Okinawa** was the last large-scale battle in the Pacific and the most intense of the island invasions. Unlike Iwo Jima, Okinawa had a large civilian population, which became one of the great tragedies of the battle.

U.S. forces began amphibious landings on April 1, 1945. Japan had more than 100,000 soldiers lying in wait in a series of fortified defensive lines. The Japanese believed that the Allied weakness would be its large fleet of naval vessels anchored offshore. As a result, they planned a massive series of **kamikaze** attacks on these ships—suicide missions in which Japanese pilots crashed their fuel- and bomb-laden planes into targets—with the goal of destroying the ships or forcing them to abandon their troops on land. However, these kamikaze attacks did not do nearly as much damage as the Japanese had anticipated, and the U.S. fleet was able to remain in place and continue to offer air support to the troops on the ground.

The battle lasted for two and a half months, until June 21, and cost nearly 19,000 American lives. The Japanese losses were even more sobering: more than 100,000 Japanese soldiers were killed, while the civilian death toll was estimated to be 80,000 to 100,000.

MOUNTING CASUALTIES

As Allied forces retook one by one the territories that Japan had captured earlier in the war, they became alarmed by Japan's increasingly extreme tactics. At Guadalcanal in August 1942 and in nearly every battle afterward, Japanese forces simply refused to surrender, even when they were clearly losing. This tactic resulted in huge death tolls for the Japanese forces, as well as increased Allied casualties. Each battle became progressively worse in this respect, and by the battles of Iwo Jima and Okinawa in 1945, the Japanese were fighting to nearly the last man. In Okinawa, even many Japanese civilians committed suicide when it became clear that the island was falling to the Americans.

These developments made Allied commanders worry about what it would take to win the war. Although the Allies had a plan in the works to land U.S. ground troops on the Japanese home islands, if the Japanese population chose to fight to the death, as many were speculating, the cost in American lives would be overwhelming. As Allied forces closed in on Japan proper, however, the U.S. Air Force was able to stage extensive bombing raids over Japanese cities, including Tokyo, which gradually began to demonstrate a viable alternative to a ground invasion.

SUMMARY & ANALYSIS

NORTH AFRICA AND THE INVASION OF ITALY

EVENTS

January 12, 1941	Britain captures Tobruk, Libya
June 21, 1942	Germans retake Tobruk
October 23	Battle of El-Alamein begins
November 8	Operation Torch; joint U.S.-British landing in French North Africa
November 11	Britain retakes Tobruk
November 25	Allies begin offensive into Tunisia
March 7, 1943	Tunis falls to Allied forces
July 10	Allied invasion of Sicily (Operation Husky) begins
July 22	Palermo falls to Allies
July 24	Mussolini is overthrown in a peaceful coup
September 2	Allied invasion of Italy begins
September 8	Italy surrenders to Allies
October 1	Allies capture Naples
May 18, 1944	Monte Cassino falls to Allies
June 5	Rome falls to Allies

KEY PEOPLE

Erwin Rommel	German tank commander whose strategic skill and surprise attacks earned him the nickname "Desert Fox"
Benito Mussolini	Italian dictator whose ill-advised military offensives embroiled Italian and German forces in North Africa; was deposed by coup in July 1943

TOBRUK

At the same time that war was going on in the European and Pacific theaters, conflict also escalated in **North Africa**, primarily as a result of **Italy**'s aggression in the region in 1940 and 1941. One of the primary flash points in North Africa was the key port of **Tobruk**, Libya, which changed hands between the Germans and the British several times and was the site of several major battles.

Originally in Italy's sphere of influence, Tobruk fell to the British on January 12, 1941, building upon the initiative they had seized after Italy's defeat in Egypt the previous year. More than a year later, in June 1942, Tobruk fell to the Germans after a long and intensive siege by Field Marshal **Erwin Rommel**'s tank forces. Then, in November 1942, Tobruk fell once more to the British and remained under their control for the rest of the war.

EL-ALAMEIN

Perhaps the most decisive battle in North Africa was the **Battle of El-Alamein**, from October 23 to November 3, 1942, in which a powerful British offensive defeated German forces overwhelmingly. The British outnumbered the Germans two to one, and Rommel, who had by this time earned the nickname "Desert Fox" for his brilliant surprise attacks, was away on sick leave when the battle began. As the battle started, Rommel's substitute died of a heart attack, and by the time Rommel arrived, the situation was hopeless.

OPERATION TORCH

Within days of the British victory at El-Alamein, the Allies launched **Operation Torch**, the code name for their invasion of North Africa. On November 8, 1942, British and American forces carried out an amphibious landing on the coast of **French North Africa** (present-day Morocco). The invasion involved more than 100,000 men and over 600 ships, placing it among the largest such invasions in history. Operation Torch was highly successful and enabled the Allies to take more than 1,000 miles of North African coastline.

TUNISIA

With Operation Torch completed and many Allied troops on the ground in Africa, the Allies energetically pursued the Axis forces that had begun retreating into **Tunisia**. The desert terrain in Tunisia was ideal for a defending force, and it was here that Rommel planned to make a stand against the Allies. The Allies did not begin their offensive into Tunisia until November 25, 1942, however, and the delay of several weeks gave Germany and Italy time to airlift more troops and equipment to the region. Thus, by the time U.S. and British forces began their attacks, the Axis forces substantially outnumbered them.

The Allies faced a difficult challenge in Tunisia, and their progress was very slow. Rommel's forces fought with tenacity in one battle after another as the fighting continued well into the spring of 1943. Nonetheless, the Allies did consistently gain ground on the Axis forces. On May 7, the Allies took Tunis and soon took the remaining Axis forces in Africa—more than 200,000 in all—prisoner. With that, the war in North Africa was over.

RESULTS OF THE NORTH AFRICAN CAMPAIGN

The war in North Africa was essentially an adventure initiated by Italy in an attempt to seize former colonial territories of Britain and France. As it became apparent that the Italian military had taken on more than it could handle, Germany was forced to come to Italy's defense. In that respect, the campaign in North Africa was very much like the failed Italian campaign in Greece in November 1940. Unlike Greece, however, North Africa was a large-scale conflict and forced Hitler to divert considerable resources, severely weakening German efforts elsewhere. Ultimately, the North Africa campaign was a serious defeat for the Axis powers. It also marked the first major involvement in the European theater by U.S. forces.

OPERATION HUSKY

Following the Axis defeat in North Africa, the Allies pursued them to the island of **Sicily**. On July 10, 1943, U.S. and British forces began **Operation Husky**, an invasion of the island using troops deployed by gliders, parachutes, and boats. Many of these landings were disrupted by high winds, making it difficult for Allied troops to regroup once on the ground. During the first few days, the invaders encountered significant resistance around Sicily's main airfield, but it was quickly overcome. On July 22, the Sicilian capital of Palermo fell to the Allies, and Sicily was secured.

THE INVASION OF THE ITALIAN MAINLAND

The day after the fall of Sicily, Italy's Fascist ruler, **Benito Mussolini,** was overthrown by a peaceful coup, and Italian officials promptly began approaching the Allies about an armistice. Prior to Mussolini's ouster, U.S. and British forces had planned an invasion of the Italian mainland, and the sudden turn of events took the Allied leaders by surprise. Although Italy officially surrendered to the Allies on September 8, 1943, the Allied invasion of Italy proceeded as planned, as there were still a large number of German forces stationed in the country.

Following the success in North Africa, British forces landed at **Taranto,** on the southeastern tip of Italy, on September 2. However, the main invasion did not begin until September 9, the day after Italy's surrender. The two forces planned to fight their way across the country to meet in the middle. German resistance proved very heavy, however, and the U.S. forces in particular suffered great casualties. After slow and treacherous fighting, the Allies finally captured the port of **Naples** on October 1, putting all of southern Italy under Allied control.

MONTE CASSINO AND ROME

Even though the Italian government had surrendered, the Germans were determined not to allow **Rome** to fall to the Allies. As the Allies secured their position in southern Italy, German forces formed a defensive line across the width of Italy, just south of Rome. This barrier was called the **Winter Line** and stretched from one coast of Italy to the other, crossing the center of the country at the fortified monastery of **Monte Cassino**.

The heavily defended Winter Line presented a very formidable obstacle to the Allied forces, who assaulted the entrenched Germans over and over again and each time were pushed back. The stalemate persisted for more than six months until Monte Cassino finally fell on May 18, 1944. Rome was liberated shortly thereafter, on June 5. The Germans retreated a short distance and formed a new defensive line in northern Italy, the **Gothic Line**, which would hold until the spring of 1945.

ITALY'S ROLE IN THE WAR

In sum, Italy's participation in World War II provided little strategic benefit for Germany; in fact, it actually hindered the German war effort by diverting German forces from more important tasks. All of Italy's actions were undertaken at the whim of its dictator, Mussolini, whose decisions became so erratic and potentially costly that his own underlings eventually decided to overthrow him. Indeed, the battles that resulted from Italy's initially frivolous and aimless campaigns became increasingly devastating. The campaign in North Africa ballooned into a huge endeavor that cost tens of thousands of lives, and the battles on the Italian mainland between Allied and German forces proved even more devastating.

The German Retreat from Russia

Events

July 5, 1943	Battle of Kursk begins
July 12	Germany retreats from Kursk
September 25	Soviet forces liberate Smolensk
November 6	Soviet forces liberate Kiev
January 27, 1944	Siege of Leningrad is broken
June 22	Russian offensive through Belorussia (Operation Bagration) begins
July 3	Soviet forces liberate Minsk
July 24	Soviet forces capture Majdanek extermination camp in Poland

The Germans Post-Stalingrad

After the devastation of the Battle of Stalingrad, which ended in February 1943, the Soviets and Germans took more than four months to regroup. Though forced to abandon the Caucasus region, the Germans continued to hold the Ukraine, with their forces concentrated to the west of the city of **Kursk** in western Russia. Hitler, determined to avenge his humiliating defeat at Stalingrad, formulated a plan known as **Operation Citadel**. Both the Germans and Soviets built up heavy armor, artillery, and air forces prior to the attack. The Soviets also created an incredible line of trenches, mines, and anti-tank barriers to slow the Germans.

The Battle of Kursk

The clash between German and Soviet forces began on the night of July 4, 1943, on a 200-mile front with a total of roughly 5,000 tanks and 4,000 aircraft in place—one of the largest armored conflicts in history. The Germans proved surprisingly effective at removing and neutralizing the Soviet minefields. After several days of escalation, the central episode of the battle took place on July 12 at the village of Prokhorovka, where nearly 2,000 tanks clashed at once.

In sharp contrast to Stalingrad, the **Battle of Kursk** was over in only a few weeks. By July 14, Germany was in retreat, with the Soviets pursuing them close behind. On August 5, the Soviets liberated the city of Orel, which lay to the north of Kursk, closing another major gap in the front. From this point forward, the USSR had the initiative and commenced a long offensive push that would slowly drive the Germans back to the west.

SOVIET VICTORIES IN THE UKRAINE

During the late summer and autumn of 1943, the Soviets advanced steadily, achieving a series of victories as they pushed the Germans westward across the **Ukraine**. The first major victory came on August 22, when the Red Army retook the city of Kharkov. Meanwhile, the Germans were planning the construction of a massive defensive wall all the way from the Gulf of Finland in the north to the Sea of Azov in the south. To be called the **Panther Line**, it was meant to be analogous to the Atlantic Wall that the Germans were building near Normandy, France (*see* The Allied Invasion of France, *p. 59*). The wall was never built, however, for the Soviets advanced too quickly for the construction site to be held.

On September 25, Stalin's forces retook the city of **Smolensk**, which was a keystone in Germany's defense effort. Dnepropetrovsk fell on October 25, followed by the Ukrainian capital of **Kiev** on November 6. Germany's southern army group was now in full-scale retreat and would be expelled from Soviet territory early in 1944.

THE END OF THE SIEGE OF LENINGRAD

The city of **Leningrad**, meanwhile, was still starving under the crippling German siege that had begun all the way back in September 1941 (*see* Kiev and Leningrad, *p. 30*). The city was completely encircled by German troops, aside from a sliver of land that allowed access to nearby Lake Ladoga. Although the situation for those trapped in the city was grim, Russians were able to get some food and medical supplies into the city via trucks driving across the frozen lake. The task was dangerous, as many trucks fell victim to German shelling or broke through the ice and sank, but the supplies helped Leningrad's population endure the Germans' brutally long siege.

On January 27, 1944, the siege of Leningrad was finally broken, roughly 900 days after it had begun. The combined forces of the Red Army pushing in from the outside and Soviet troops and resistance fighters pushing out from the inside broke the German siege line. Within days, the German forces surrounding the city were forced out of the Leningrad region entirely.

The liberation of Leningrad was a tremendous victory for the Soviets, both literally and symbolically. More than 600,000 Russians died from starvation, exposure, or disease during the siege, and the rest were kept alive only barely by the supplies delivered across Lake Ladoga. Throughout the siege, Soviet forces trapped within the city had stood firm and prevented German forces from ever entering.

GERMAN ATROCITIES

With the Leningrad siege broken, all German forces on Soviet territory, except for the Crimea, were in active retreat during early 1944. With each passing month, more and more Soviet cities and towns were liberated, and the Germans lost more and more of the ground they had seized in 1941 and 1942. The retreat was nonetheless brutal as the Germans stepped up their murder campaigns to a frenzy. As the Nazi forces abandoned their positions, they executed any remaining Jewish slave laborers and Soviet prisoners, along with anyone even remotely suspected of partisan involvement. In Belorussia, entire towns were burned to the ground together with their residents.

OPERATION BAGRATION

Although the Red Army kept pushing, it was not until the summer of 1944 that a major Soviet offensive took place. **Operation Bagration** began three years to the day after Germany's initial invasion of Russia, on June 22, 1944. The objective was to drive out completely the German forces centered in Belorussia and central Russia. The Soviets advanced with nearly 2 million troops and thousands of tanks and within days had broken the German front line in two. On July 3, Soviet forces took the Belorussian capital of **Minsk**, and less than two weeks later, the Red Army reached the Polish border.

THE DISCOVERY OF CONCENTRATION CAMPS

As the Red Army advanced west into Europe via Poland, Slovakia, and Romania, they uncovered a growing body of evidence concerning German atrocities. On July 24, 1944, Soviet soldiers moving through Lublin, Poland, captured the Majdanek **extermination camp** before its German operators could destroy the evidence of what had taken place there. Upon arrival, they found hundreds of dead bodies, along with gas chambers, crematoria, and thousands of living prisoners in varying states of starvation. Although the West had received reports of such atrocities for some time, this Soviet discovery was the first absolute proof.

THE POLISH INSURGENCY

At the same time, an active **Polish insurgency** continued to fight against the Germans in Warsaw and throughout western Poland.

The Allies had limited success in their efforts to airdrop supplies and other means of support to these insurgents. The Soviet government refused to assist in these airdrops and even actively discouraged them, claiming that they would have negligible effect on the war and were a waste of time. However, as the Red Army made its way deeper into Poland, Stalin's intentions became clearer, as reports surfaced in the West that Soviets "liberating" Polish territory were actually arresting members of the Polish insurgency in large numbers.

GERMANY ON THE DEFENSIVE

Germany's defeat at Kursk in July 1943 was almost simultaneous with the Allied invasion of Sicily, and Hitler was forced to withdraw some generals and forces to fight the new threat in Italy. This **multi-front war** began to take a serious toll on Germany's capability to control the territory it had seized over the previous four years. As Soviet forces advanced farther west during early 1944, the German military leadership also had to prepare for the expected British and American invasion of France. Consequently, Germany withdrew still more forces from the collapsing eastern front. Although Hitler was still far from giving up, his conquests were clearly in decline and his war machine gradually collapsing.

THE ALLIED INVASION OF FRANCE

EVENTS

June 6, 1944	D-Day invasion begins
July 20	Attempt on Hitler's life nearly succeeds
Late July	Allied forces make first significant inland progress
August 15	Allies forces land on Mediterranean coast of France
Mid-August	Hitler orders evacuation of southern France Soviet forces enter Germany from the east
August 30	Soviet forces capture Ploesti, Romania
September 10	First Allied troops enter Germany from west
October 18	Hitler authorizes conscription of all healthy men aged 16–60

KEY PEOPLE

Dwight D. Eisenhower U.S. general and supreme commander of Allied forces in western Europe; planned Normandy invasion

OPERATION OVERLORD

By early 1944, the Allies, under the leadership of U.S. general **Dwight D. Eisenhower,** had been planning an invasion of **France** for more than a year. The Germans, anticipating such an invasion since 1942, had begun building the **Atlantic Wall,** a series of heavily armed fortifications all along the French coast. As the Allied invasion plan became more specific, it was dubbed **Operation Overlord,** and preparations and training for the mission began in earnest.

As part of the invasion plan, the Allies instigated a mass disinformation campaign in hopes of directing German forces away from the actual landing point. As part of this effort, the Allies made use of German spies in Britain who had been turned and were serving as double agents. These double agents helped convince the German leadership that the invasion would take place near **Calais,** the point where the English Channel was narrowest, when in fact the invasion was targeted farther south, in **Normandy.**

D-DAY

The invasion was launched early in the morning of June 6, 1944—the famous **D-Day**—barely a day after U.S. troops had liberated the Italian capital of Rome. Overnight, roughly 20,000 British and American airborne troops had been dropped by parachute and glider a short distance inland of the Normandy coast, ordered to do as much damage as possible to the German fortified coastal defenses. Meanwhile, over 6,000 ships were making their way across the English Channel to deliver a huge expeditionary force onto five separate beaches between Cherbourg and Caen. The first wave alone brought 150,000 Allied soldiers to the French shore, and over the coming weeks, more than 2 million more would enter France via the Normandy beaches—to this day the largest seaborne invasion in history. Opposing the invaders were thousands of German troops manning the fortifications above the beaches.

The first day of the invasion was costly for the Allies in terms of casualties—especially at one landing point, **Omaha Beach**—but the Germans were vastly outnumbered and rapidly overwhelmed by the incoming forces. The German high command still believed that a larger invasion was imminent at Calais or elsewhere, so they withheld reserve forces in the area from moving against the Normandy invaders. The Allies therefore accomplished nearly all of their set objectives for the first day, which included fully securing the landing areas.

The Battle of Normandy

Breaking out of the Normandy coast and into inland France proved more difficult, in part because of stubbornly defended German defense posts at Cherbourg and Caen, which framed the area. The Allies were unable to advance inland in significant numbers until July 28, 1944, by which time the two German forts had been defeated. During August, the Allied forces that continued to land in Normandy were able to move rapidly into the heart of France.

Operation Dragoon

On August 15, a second Allied assault was made into France, this time along the Mediterranean coast in the south. This campaign, called **Operation Dragoon**, involved nearly 100,000 troops, who rapidly spread out northward into France. With this southern operation a success, Allied forces were able to approach the French capital from two directions.

Paris

By mid-August 1944, most of northwestern France was under Allied control, and from there, the Allied advance moved rapidly. Hitler ordered the evacuation of southern France, and German troops also began the process of evacuating **Paris** itself. At almost the same time, Soviet troops invading from the other front first crossed Germany's eastern border.

Even as it became inevitable that France would fall to the Allies, however, the Nazi war machine continued deporting French Jews to **Auschwitz** and other extermination camps without letup. A few days later, on August 25, Allied forces entered Paris, by which point all remaining German troops had either evacuated or been taken prisoner.

THE APPROACH TO GERMANY

Even though the war in Europe would continue for another seven months, September 1944 brought Germany perilously close to defeat. During that month, Allied troops overran most of France, pushed deep into **Belgium**, and were on the verge of entering the **Netherlands**. The first Allied soldier crossed into Germany on September 10; although this mission was only a brief excursion, Allied ground missions into Germany would become increasingly frequent.

After the success of Operation Overlord, the Allies had the ability to launch bomber raids from France, Italy, and Britain, which vastly expanded the range and duration of aerial attacks inside Germany. Simultaneously, the Soviets were closing in from the east: although Warsaw was still under German control, the Red Army had taken much of eastern Poland. The Soviets also had advanced into Czechoslovakia, Romania, Bulgaria, and Yugoslavia—the latter two of which even signed formal agreements of cooperation with the USSR.

GERMANY SURROUNDED

By the autumn of 1944, Germany was surrounded on all sides. Allied air strikes on German industrial facilities, particularly oil reserves, prevented the Luftwaffe from posing the serious threat that it once had. This gap in Germany's defense left the country very vulnerable to attack. Moreover, the fuel situation in Germany was becoming truly desperate, especially after the city of **Ploiesti**, Romania, fell to the Red Army on August 30. Ploiesti had been the last oil source available to Germany, as it was now cut off from the Black Sea.

Few in the German high command could have failed to recognize that they were in serious trouble, even if they could not admit it publicly. A resistance movement against Hitler grew among the German officer corps, and several attempts were made on Hitler's life throughout the summer, including a bombing on July 20 that nearly succeeded. After the failed attempt, Hitler cracked down mercilessly on known opponents, executing more than 4,000 of them.

On October 18, Hitler ordered the **conscription** of all healthy German men aged sixteen to sixty in order to defend the country from an obviously imminent invasion. Hitler intended for the country to fight to the last man and planned to employ a **scorched-earth policy** similar to the strategy the Soviets had used against Hitler's own forces in the USSR in 1941.

THE FALL OF GERMANY

S U M M A R Y   &   A N A L Y S I S

EVENTS

November 20, 1944	Hitler abandons Rastenburg headquarters
December 16	Battle of the Bulge; Germans begin counteroffensive in Ardennes
December 24	Germans surround Americans at Bastogne
January 16, 1945	U.S. forces freed from Bastogne
February 4	Roosevelt, Churchill, and Stalin meet at Yalta Conference
April 12	Roosevelt dies; Truman becomes U.S. president
April 16	Soviets begin offensive on Berlin
April 25	U.S. and Soviet advances meet for first time
April 28	Partisans execute Mussolini
April 30	Hitler commits suicide
May 7	Germany signs formal surrender
May 8	Western Allies declare V-E Day
May 9	USSR declares Victory Day

KEY PEOPLE

Adolf Hitler	German chancellor; committed suicide on April 30, 1945, with fall of Berlin imminent
Franklin D. Roosevelt	32nd U.S. president; met with Churchill and Stalin at Yalta Conference but died in April 1945
Harry S Truman	33rd U.S. president; took office upon Roosevelt's death
Winston Churchill	British prime minister; met with Roosevelt and Stalin at February 1945 Yalta Conference
Joseph Stalin	Soviet premier; began to assert USSR's dominance over Eastern Europe in final days of the war, which led to Cold War tensions

GERMAN DESPERATION

During the second half of 1944, the Nazi empire gradually imploded as its enemies invaded from east, west, and south. Supplies and manufacturing dwindled on a daily basis. The once-mighty **Luftwaffe** had some of the best military aircraft in the world but lacked fuel to fly them and parts to maintain them. Evidence suggests that Chancellor **Adolf Hitler** himself became addicted to a variety of drugs and that he may also have suffered from syphilis, Parkinson's disease, or both.

Far separated from reality, Hitler placed his last hope of winning the war on the latest developments of German technology. These developments were both impressive and real but were too late and too poorly executed to change the outcome of the war or even delay it by much. Among Germany's most fearsome new weapons were two **missiles**, the V1 and the V2. The V1 was the world's first cruise missile, the V2 the world's first weaponized ballistic missile. Other German innovations included both jet- and rocket-propelled aircraft. However, nearly all of these innovations were still experimental in nature and not truly ready for effective use in combat. German scientists were also busily working on the development of an **atomic bomb**, but the war ended before they could succeed.

THE BATTLE OF THE BULGE

On December 16, 1944, the Germans began their last major counteroffensive of the war, as three German armies surged into the Ardennes Forest, dividing the Allied front with the ultimate goal of retaking the Belgian city of Antwerp. This time, Allied intelligence failed to intercept the German plans, and the action was a complete surprise.

The Germans launched the attack during a heavy snowstorm that grounded all aircraft, making it difficult for the Allies to evaluate the extent of the attack. Furthermore, the Germans deployed a group of about thirty English-speaking soldiers behind Allied lines, dressed in American uniforms and driving captured American vehicles. These special troops succeeded in creating chaos among the Allied troops by reversing road signs, cutting communications wires, and inciting a panic among Allied troops once they realized that they had been infiltrated.

By December 24, the Germans had penetrated deep into French territory, making a distinct bulge in the front line that lent the **Battle of the Bulge** its name. German forces surrounded a large contingent of U.S forces in the town of Bastogne and attempted to intimidate them with an invitation of surrender. The offer was refused.

As the weather cleared and Allied aircraft could fly again, the Germans were pushed back, and supplies were airdropped to the trapped American troops. In the meantime, other Allied armies were diverted from other areas of France to help. By early January 1945, the Germans were once again in retreat, and on January 16, the soldiers trapped at Bastogne were free, and the "bulge" was no more.

THE GERMAN RETREAT FROM THE EAST

Throughout the fall and winter of 1944, Soviet forces slowly but steadily made their way toward Germany through eastern Europe. The brunt of the assault was concentrated on **Poland**, where most of the Nazis' **concentration camps** were located. By early November 1944, the German **S.S.** was trying frantically to dismantle these camps and hide evidence of the atrocities that had taken place. The

Nazis forced those prisoners who were still living to march on foot westward to Germany. On November 20, Hitler himself retreated, abandoning his staff headquarters at Rastenburg along the Polish-German border and relocating to **Berlin**.

THE YALTA CONFERENCE

On February 4, 1945, Franklin D. Roosevelt, Winston Churchill, and Joseph Stalin came together for a now-famous meeting at **Yalta**, a resort on the Crimean Peninsula in the USSR. During the meeting, the "Big Three," as they came to be called, discussed their strategy for the last stages of the war. They agreed that Britain and the United States would provide bomber support for Soviet troops fighting along the eastern front.

The three leaders also spoke about the issue of how Europe would be divided after the war, with particular concern regarding the situation in **Poland**, which was by this point controlled entirely by the Soviet Union. With considerable difficulty, Roosevelt and Churchill managed to pressure Stalin into holding democratic elections in Poland. However, these turned out to be heavily rigged in favor of a pro-Soviet Communist government.

THE SOVIET ADVANCE

Meanwhile, the Red Army had moved deep into **Hungary** and, by early December, had taken most of the country except for the area immediately around Budapest. U.S. and British aircraft provided support as the Soviets advanced into German territory, making devastating bombing attacks on the cities of Leipzig, Dresden, and Berlin. Dresden, in particular, was almost completely destroyed.

By late March 1945, the Red Army had secured all of eastern Europe. It continued its advance into **Austria**, capturing the capital of **Vienna** on April 13. By this time, the Allied forces coming from France had crossed the Rhine River and were moving swiftly toward Berlin from the west. The Allies decided to let Soviet forces enter Berlin first, while British and U.S. forces concentrated on other areas to the north and south.

ROOSEVELT'S DEATH

On April 12, 1945, U.S. president **Franklin D. Roosevelt**, whose health had been failing for some time, died of a cerebral hemorrhage at his vacation home in Georgia. The United States saw an outpouring of grief, as Roosevelt had been president an unprecedented twelve years and, in addition to being an effective commander in chief and diplomatic leader, had almost single-handedly rallied the American people through the hardships of the war. Vice President **Harry S Truman** succeeded Roosevelt as president.

THE END OF NAZI GERMANY

Just days after Roosevelt's death, on April 16, 1945, the Soviets began their final offensive against the Third Reich. Over the coming days, more than 3,000 tanks crossed the Neisse River, assaulting Berlin's outer defenses while Allied aircraft bombed the city from above. On April 20, Hitler spent his birthday in an underground bunker and soon resigned to kill himself when the city fell. Although imminent defeat was obvious, Hitler not only refused to allow his troops to surrender but also insisted that the conscripted civilian army was to defend Berlin to the last man.

On April 25, the Allied armies advancing from east and west met for the first time, when a small group of American and Soviet soldiers met at the German village of Stehla. The hugely symbolic meeting was marked by celebrations in both Moscow and New York. On April 28, the former dictator of Italy, **Benito Mussolini**, under arrest since his ouster nearly two years before, was executed by Italian partisans and hung upside down in the center of Milan. Two days later, on April 30, **Adolf Hitler** killed himself in the bunker in which he had been living since the beginning of the month. Later that evening, the Red Army hung a Soviet flag from the top of the **Reichstag**, the German parliament building in Berlin.

Over the following days, there was a great deal of confusion throughout Germany. Some German forces surrendered, while others continued to fight. Among the remaining leaders, some went into hiding or sought escape abroad. Others followed Hitler's example and committed suicide.

THE FORMAL SURRENDER

Early on the morning of May 7, 1945, General **Alfred Jodl** signed the official surrender on behalf of all German forces, which went into effect the next day. Some sporadic fighting continued in the interim, particularly in Czechoslovakia. During the course of May 8, nearly all remaining German forces surrendered, and that night, additional members of the German high command signed a formal surrender. The Western Allies thus celebrated May 8, 1945, as **V-E Day** (Victory in Europe Day). Because some fighting between Soviet and German forces continued into the next day, May 9 became the official **Victory Day** in the USSR.

THE SEEDS OF THE COLD WAR

As it turned out, the dividing line between the Red Army's position and the Western Allied armies' position at the end of the war in Europe would solidify into roughly the same line as the **Iron Curtain,** the line dividing Western Europe from Eastern Europe in the Cold War. Berlin itself would remain divided into Soviet and Western zones—which became East and West Berlin, respectively—for decades. (*For more information, see the History SparkNote* The Cold War.)

THE FALL OF JAPAN

EVENTS

March 1945	Allies begin mass bombing raids of Tokyo and other cities
July 16	United States successfully tests first atomic bomb
July 26	Potsdam Declaration signed
August 6	United States drops atomic bomb on Hiroshima
August 8	USSR enters war against Japan
August 9	United States drops atomic bomb on Nagasaki USSR invades Manchuria
August 15	Hirohito announces Japan's surrender
September 2	Japan signs formal surrender

KEY PEOPLE

Harry S Truman	33rd U.S. president; after death of Roosevelt, made decision to drop atomic bombs on Hiroshima and Nagasaki in August 1945
Curtis LeMay	U.S. general who orchestrated brutal incendiary bombing campaign against major Japanese cities in March 1945

THE TOKYO AIR RAIDS

During the same months that Allied forces in Europe were closing in on Germany, Allied forces in the Pacific were closing in on **Japan**. In March 1945, the U.S. Air Force began a series of heavy bombing campaigns against major Japanese cities. These attacks were the brainchild of General **Curtis LeMay**, who headed the 21st Bomber Command. The operations used America's new strategic bomber, the **B-29**, and directly targeted the Japanese civilian population in addition to industrial and military targets. The strategy was simply to destroy the Japanese will to resist.

Many of these raids were conducted on the capital of **Tokyo** itself, though other cities such as Kobe were also hit. In the spring and summer of 1945, the severity of these air raids grew exponentially, some causing firestorms that produced death tolls in the hundreds of thousands. By late summer, little of Tokyo and the other targeted cities were left standing.

THE POTSDAM DECLARATION

Between July 17 and August 2, 1945, **Harry S Truman** of the United States, **Winston Churchill** of Britain (and later Clement Atlee, who replaced him as prime minister during the conference), and **Joseph Stalin** of the USSR met in Potsdam, Germany, with other Allied leaders to discuss the future administration of Germany. On July 26, the three also held a special meeting to settle on the terms of surrender for Japan in order to end the war. The agreement was set forth in a document known as the **Potsdam Declaration**. In short, it demanded an unconditional surrender that included the complete demilitarization of the country and the replacement of Japan's current leadership by a "peacefully inclined and responsible government."

THE MANHATTAN PROJECT

During the summer of 1945, American scientists succeeded in completing a working **atomic bomb**, which was tested a single time, on July 16, at a remote location in New Mexico. Scientists around the world had theorized about the concept of such a weapon for years, and active research on its development had been taking place not only in the United States but also in Nazi Germany, Japan, and the USSR. The American effort, which was conducted with substantial help from Canada and Britain, was code-named the **Manhattan Project**. Shortly after the July test, the Truman administration began seriously to consider using the bomb against Japan. Eventually, Truman made the difficult decision to do so, in spite of considerable resistance from U.S. military leaders. Despite the fact that the bomb would kill tens of thousands of innocents, Truman felt that it would ultimately save both U.S. military and Japanese civilian casualties that would inevitably result from a ground invasion of Japan.

HIROSHIMA AND NAGASAKI

The first atomic bomb was dropped from a B-29 called the *Enola Gay* on the morning of August 6, 1945, onto the city of **Hiroshima**. The blast obliterated most of the central city, killing 80,000 in a single moment. By the end of the year, 60,000 more victims would die from radiation poisoning, and thousands more would die in the years to come, from cancer and other long-term effects of the radiation. It is estimated that the total death toll from Hiroshima was well over 200,000.

The immediate reaction to the bomb in Japan was one of total incomprehension. All communications with Hiroshima were lost, and rumors quickly spread that the city had vanished in some kind of cataclysmic explosion. Yet Japanese military radar had indicated that only a few isolated planes had been in the area. The Japanese would learn the truth sixteen hours following the explosion, when the U.S. government released a public statement explaining what had taken place. Three days later, on August 9, a second atomic bomb was dropped on the port city of **Nagasaki** with similarly devastating results.

JAPAN SURRENDERS

The day before the Nagasaki bombing, the Soviet Union entered the war against Japan and commenced an attack on the Chinese province of Manchuria, which was still held by the Japanese. The combination of the atomic bombings with the potential threat of a full-scale invasion of Japan by the USSR was enough to remove any hope that Japan may have held for continuing the war. On August 15, 1945, Emperor **Hirohito** announced Japan's capitulation in accordance with the Potsdam Declaration. A **formal surrender** was signed on September 2 aboard the battleship USS *Missouri*.

TRUMAN'S DECISION

The campaign against Japan at the end of the war and the use of the atomic bomb have long been the subject of debate and controversy around the world, especially outside the United States. Critics contend that Japan was already on the verge of surrender by late summer 1945 and that the atomic bombings were superfluous, needlessly killing hundreds of thousands of people. The same was said about the mass incendiary bombing attacks on Tokyo and other cities, which killed even more people than did the atomic bombs, although without as many long-term effects.

On the other hand, proponents of the bombings say that battles such as Iwo Jima and Okinawa demonstrated that the Japanese population was prepared to fight to the last man and that only a weapon as overpowering as the atomic bomb could have ended the war without unfathomable casualties. Indeed, the only alternative to the bombings would have been a ground invasion using U.S. troops, which would have been extremely costly in both American and Japanese lives. The argument has thus been made that such a ground invasion would have cost far more Japanese lives than the Nagasaki and Hiroshima bombings combined.

Moreover, evidence suggests that external political factors played a significant part in the decision to drop the atomic bombs. The Manhattan Project had been very expensive, and the Truman administration felt pressured to demonstrate that the weapon actually could be used effectively for military purposes. Furthermore, tensions were growing with the Soviet Union over the division of Eastern Europe, and the United States may have wished to demonstrate its newfound power.

Finally, the atomic bomb was a new, untested technology. The worldwide cultural taboo surrounding such weapons did not exist at the time, and in general there was less understanding of the long-term effects of their use—only one atomic bomb had ever been tested successfully. Frighteningly, as powerful as the Hiroshima and Nagasaki bombs were, their destructive power was small in comparison with the nuclear weapons of today.

SUMMARY & ANALYSIS

STUDY QUESTIONS & ESSAY TOPICS

Always use specific historical examples to support your arguments.

STUDY QUESTIONS

1. *Compare the roles of Germany and Japan during World War II. Generally speaking, were their aggressions fundamentally similar or fundamentally different?*

The respective roles of Germany and Japan in the initiation and escalation of World War II seem similar on the surface—a combination of economic ambition and racist ideology. However, the countries' root motivations and the ways in which they were expressed were fundamentally different.

Both Germany and Japan engaged in large-scale territorial conquests in the years leading up to World War II. Hitler and other Nazi officials in Germany advocated the concept of *lebensraum*, the natural "living space" required by what they considered the racially superior German people. Under this doctrine, Hitler claimed openly that German territory needed to be expanded through conquest of surrounding nations. Though some of Japan's leaders held similar beliefs in the racial superiority of the Japanese people, they also had concrete motivations for territorial expansion: Japan's population was growing too large for the confines of the Japanese islands, and colonial holdings in Asia were arguably becoming necessary to feed and clothe the Japanese people.

Also, Japan's economic problems were far more severe than Germany's. Although the German people were indeed humiliated by the terms of the Treaty of Versailles that ended World War I, Germany actually ended up *not* paying the bulk of the economic reparations that the treaty demanded. Rather, Hitler channeled the German people's resentment to fuel his own schemes. Japan, however, though a victor in World War I, suffered when the United States and several European nations imposed high tariffs and blocked industrial imports. As a result, many Japanese people began to believe that whites were hostile to the idea of a developed non-white nation.

In response, Japan's leaders asserted the superiority of their people and tried to change Japan into a colonial power itself, rather than a colonial subject. They therefore invaded and attempted to "develop" other Asian countries, including China and Korea. However, though Japanese policies in these countries were sometimes brutal, and often motivated by ideas of racial superiority, they were a far cry from the overtly genocidal goals of the Nazi death camps.

Ultimately, whereas Japan's racist ideology and territorial ambitions grew as a result of real economic problems and Western exclusion, Hitler used Germany's alleged economic woes and residual resentment from the Treaty of Versailles to promote his own racist ideas and premeditated plan to expand Germany's borders.

2. *Consider the role of technology during World War II. Did it fundamentally affect the outcome of the war? If so, how? If not, why not?*

World War II saw the new application of many new technologies by military forces on all sides of the conflict, and some of them had a profound impact on the war. The airplane in particular became a fundamental instrument of war and changed the way many battles were fought. Much the same may be said of the aircraft carrier, which became crucial to the United States after so many of its battleships were lost at Pearl Harbor. As a result of these developments, the Battle of Britain in 1940 marked the first time in history when air power alone determined the course of a major battle, and the Battle of the Coral Sea in 1942 was the first naval battle in history fought exclusively in the air, by carrier-based planes. Both sides also realized the effectiveness of radar as a way of warning against approaching enemy planes. Germany experimented with new missile technologies as well as both jet- and rocket-powered aircraft, but none of these projects was perfected in time to change the outcome of the war.

Although the majority of these new technologies had an effect on the war, they generally were created by one side in response to similar technologies being developed by the other side—the net effect of which was to balance out the new power these technologies offered. The notable exception was the atomic bomb, which the United States developed in secret from 1942 to 1945 and which Japan had no way to counter at the time. Indeed, Japan declared its surrender just days after the bombs were dropped on Hiroshima and Nagasaki in August 1945. Even today, however, historians debate whether the atomic bomb changed the outcome of the war, as Japan may have been already very close to surrendering.

3. *Explain Germany's mistakes in Russia and the ways in which they affected the outcome of the war.*

Most historians concur that Hitler's decision to invade the Soviet Union was one of the primary causes of Germany's ultimate defeat. By invading the USSR, Germany made essentially the same mistake that Japan made by expanding so far across the Pacific. The huge expanse of the Soviet Union and the vast distances between its major cities required an enormous German invasion force. Despite this geographical challenge, Hitler assumed that Operation Barbarossa would take only six months, expecting Russia to capitulate rapidly after the shock of Germany's initial, devastating attack. When events transpired differently, the German forces were faced with an enormous challenge, as their forces were dispersed and poorly equipped to deal with the brutal Russian winter. Russian soldiers and civilians, conversely, had plenty of room to retreat east when necessary, which caused the pursuing Germans to extend their supply lines so far that they were unable to maintain them. It was under these conditions that the Germans had to fight the massive battles of Stalingrad and Kursk. After the Germans lost both of these battles, they were no longer capable of maintaining their position and were forced to retreat to the west. Within a matter of months, the pursuing Red Army had pushed the Germans back through eastern Europe and toward a last stand on their home turf, which was the beginning of the end of the Nazi empire.

Suggested Essay Topics

---

1. *How and why was Germany allowed to annex Austria and the Sudetenland? Was there any justification for Britain and France's policy of appeasement?*

2. *Discuss the role that Italy played in World War II. How did the nation become involved in the conflict? How did its participation affect the direction of the war and Germany's fortunes?*

3. *Discuss the issues surrounding the United States' decision to use atomic bombs against Japan. What motives were behind this action, and what arguments have been made against it?*

4. *Explain how the situation in Europe immediately following the fall of Germany led directly to the Cold War. In your opinion, should the Western Allies have acted to oppose Soviet domination of Eastern Europe?*

Review & Resources

Quiz

1. Which event is generally considered to be the first belligerent act of World War II?

   A. Germany's attack on Russia
   B. Germany's attack on Britain
   C. Germany's attack on Poland
   D. Germany's occupation of Austria

2. Which two countries were the first to declare war on Germany?

   A. Italy and Greece
   B. Britain and France
   C. Norway and Denmark
   D. The United States and the USSR

3. Against which country did the Soviet Union instigate an armed conflict in late 1939?

   A. Finland
   B. Yugoslavia
   C. Czechoslovakia
   D. Hungary

4. What were the first two western European countries that Germany invaded?

   A. France and Belgium
   B. Norway and Denmark
   C. Switzerland and Liechtenstein
   D. Austria and the Netherlands

5. Which best describes Germany's standard invasion strategy at the beginning of World War II?

   A. Attack with a combination of speed and overwhelming force
   B. Intimidate the enemy by first amassing a large force along the enemy's border
   C. Begin with acts of sabotage behind enemy lines
   D. Draw out battles for as long as possible to wear the enemy out

6. What major mistake did the Allies make in preparing to defend against Germany's attack on France?

   A. They failed to anticipate that the attack would take place
   B. They expected an attack by ground forces rather than a naval assault
   C. They misinterpreted where the main invasion would take place
   D. They failed to set up minefields along the border with Germany

7. What happened at Dunkirk in May 1940?

   A. British forces retreated across the English Channel
   B. The French army lost a major battle
   C. American forces invaded France
   D. German forces were defeated in a large naval battle

8. Where was the French surrender to Germany signed?

   A. In Paris
   B. In Berlin
   C. In a railway car
   D. On a boat

REVIEW & RESOURCES

9. Why did the British Royal Navy attack French warships at Mers-el-Kebir?

   A. The French crews had sworn allegiance to Germany
   B. France was at war with Britain
   C. The French crews refused to surrender their ships when the British requested
   D. They were manned by Germans

10. What was Germany's initial strategy for conquering Britain?

   A. First establish air superiority, then send in ground forces
   B. First destroy the British navy, then send in ground forces
   C. First send in ground forces, then attack the country with aircraft
   D. Immobilize London with poison gas attacks

11. What was the "London Blitz"?

   A. Germany's plan for a blitzkrieg on London
   B. A term used for Germany's bombing campaign on London
   C. A series of German missile attacks late in the war
   D. Code name for a secret British radar system

12. Overall, the Battle of Britain is considered to be

   A. A victory for Germany
   B. A victory for Britain
   C. A victory for neither
   D. A minor conflict

13. What was Italy's primary role in the war?

   A. It helped Germany in accomplishing its main objectives
   B. It was helpful to Britain
   C. It caused problems for Japan
   D. It distracted Germany from accomplishing its main objectives

14. What was Hitler's primary justification for invading Russia?

    A. Stalin was preparing to attack Germany
    B. Germany needed more space for its population
    C. Hitler believed that a war on two fronts would be
       to his advantage
    D. He desired revenge for the execution of Tsar
       Nicholas II

15. What was the code name given to Germany's plan to invade
    the USSR?

    A. Operation Sea Lion
    B. Operation Barbarossa
    C. Operation Wolfenstein
    D. Operation Crossbow

16. What happened to the Soviet air force during the opening
    days of the German invasion?

    A. Up to 2,000 Soviet aircraft were destroyed while still
       on the ground.
    B. Soviet pilots scored easy victories against inexperienced
       German pilots
    C. It was evacuated to Siberia
    D. The Soviet air force engaged in huge dogfights
       involving thousands of planes on each side

17. Which of the following was *not* a part of the Soviet defense
    plan against Germany?

    A. Well-organized partisan resistance
    B. A strict policy of destroying any usable resources
       before retreating
    C. The Soviets sought to lure German armies into forests,
       which they would then set on fire
    D. Major factories were disassembled and moved east

REVIEW & RESOURCES

18. On which region of the Soviet Union did Hitler place the highest priority?

    A. Ukraine and southern Russia
    B. Leningrad and northern Russia
    C. Moscow and central Russia
    D. Siberia

19. Via what route did Russians manage to send some supplies to Leningrad during the German siege of the city?

    A. A German supply line across the Black Sea
    B. An underground railroad
    C. A supply route across Lake Ladoga
    D. An airlift

20. Which country was the site of most of the Nazi extermination camps?

    A. The USSR
    B. Czechoslovakia
    C. Poland
    D. Hungary

21. How did the Western Allies respond to Germany's invasion of Russia?

    A. They sent supplies and intelligence information to the USSR
    B. They were largely indifferent to the situation in Russia
    C. They sent large numbers of troops to fight in Russia
    D. They attacked German naval forces from the Black Sea

22. What Japanese action created tension with the United States?

    A. Its seizure of territory in China
    B. Its seizure of territory in Russia
    C. Its seizure of territory in Korea
    D. Its decision to block American shipping routes

23. What U.S. action created tension with Japan?

    A. Its blockade of Japanese ports
    B. Its freezing of Japanese assets
    C. Its establishment of a trade embargo against Japan
    D. Its default on Japanese loans

24. Who was the Japanese admiral behind the Pearl Harbor attack?

    A. Hirohito
    B. Myamoto
    C. Yamamoto
    D. Matsuhito

25. Which of the following was *not* true about the Pearl Harbor attack?

    A. U.S. officials knew the day before that Japan was planning a major attack
    B. There was concern among U.S. military leaders that Peal Harbor was vulnerable to attack
    C. The Japanese painted their aircraft to look like American planes
    D. Prior to the attack, Japanese spies had verified which U.S. battleships would be in port

26. What was unique about the Doolittle Raid?

    A. The bombers were launched from an aircraft carrier
    B. It was the first raid to employ jet aircraft
    C. The bombers flew to Japan all the way from Hawaii
    D. The bombers were unmanned

27. Which battle is considered to be the turning point for the war in the Pacific?

    A. The Battle of the Coral Sea
    B. The Battle of Guadalcanal
    C. The Battle of Iwo Jima
    D. The Battle of Midway

REVIEW & RESOURCES

28. The Battle of the Coral Sea was a unique naval battle in that

   A. It was fought entirely with submarines
   B. It was fought during a typhoon
   C. It was fought entirely with carrier-based aircraft
   D. It was fought primarily at night

29. During the Battle of Midway, Japan lost

   A. Most of its battleships
   B. Most of its aircraft carriers
   C. Admiral Yamamoto
   D. Most of its Pacific Fleet

30. The Battle of Stalingrad was

   A. A clear-cut example of a blitzkrieg
   B. An easy victory for Germany
   C. One of the deadliest battles in human history
   D. Primarily a tank battle

31. Who met at Casablanca?

   A. Roosevelt and Churchill
   B. Roosevelt, Churchill, and Stalin
   C. Roosevelt, Churchill, Stalin, and Hitler
   D. Truman and Churchill

32. What was the focus of the Tehran Conference?

   A. The Allied invasion of France
   B. The war in the Pacific
   C. The Battle of Stalingrad
   D. The division of Germany after the war

33. What was the significance of Guadalcanal to Japan?

   A. The island was sacred to the Shinto religion
   B. The island offered a good position for attacking the Philippines
   C. The island was known to have oil reserves beneath it
   D. The island was in an ideal position for controlling the Solomon Islands

34. Why was the Japanese capture of Rangoon such a bitter loss for the Allies?

    A. They were worried about Rangoon historical sites
    B. As a major seaport, it was an excellent supply point
    C. Winston Churchill was born there
    D. The location was perfect for launching air strikes against Japan

35. Which statement best characterizes the series of battles in the Pacific following the Battle of Guadalcanal?

    A. With each battle, the Allies became increasingly disheartened until they finally gave up
    B. With each battle, the Japanese surrendered in large numbers
    C. With each battle, the Japanese soldiers increasingly fought to the death
    D. With each battle, civilian inhabitants of the islands joined the Allies in battle

36. What was the significance of Mt. Suribachi?

    A. It was the site of the bloodiest fighting on Okinawa
    B. It was the Japanese defense headquarters outside Tokyo
    C. It was the location where Japan was defeated in New Guinea
    D. It was the site of a major battle on Iwo Jima

37. Which country instigated the conflict in North Africa?

    A. Germany
    B. Italy
    C. Britain
    D. The United States

REVIEW & RESOURCES

38. Why did Allied forces invade Italy after it had already surrendered?

   A. German forces were still fighting in the country
   B. Italy refused to meet all of the Allied demands
   C. There was strong anti-Allied resistance among Italian partisans
   D. The Allies felt that Italy needed to be punished

39. What was Monte Cassino?

   A. A place where Allied soldiers celebrated after the fall of Rome
   B. The place where Italy's surrender was signed
   C. A large monastery in central Italy where the Germans defended Rome from Allied forces
   D. The site where Mussolini was killed

40. The Battle of Kursk is best described as

   A. Trench warfare
   B. An aerial battle
   C. Hand-to-hand combat
   D. A tank battle

41. After the Battle of Kursk, German forces

   A. Advanced deeper into southern Russia
   B. Finally entered Moscow
   C. Began a lengthy retreat back to Germany
   D. Held their position until the end of the war

42. What was the code name for the Allied invasion of Europe?

   A. Operation Barbarossa
   B. Operation Watchtower
   C. Operation Overlord
   D. Operation Bagration

43. The Allied invasion of Europe was primarily directed at

    A. The German coast
    B. The Italian coast
    C. The Danish coast
    D. The French coast

44. What was the location of the second major Allied assault into Europe in 1945?

    A. The Italian coast
    B. Greece
    C. The French Mediterranean coast
    D. The German North Sea coast

45. Why was the Luftwaffe so ineffective during the last part of the war?

    A. Germany was experiencing a severe oil shortage
    B. Germany was running out of pilots
    C. Most of Germany's airplanes had already been destroyed
    D. The Allies had developed a way to interfere with German navigation equipment

46. Where did the Battle of the Bulge take place?

    A. The Ardennes Forest
    B. In northern Italy, near Milan
    C. Normandy
    D. In northern Germany, near Hamburg

47. What were the V1 and V2?

    A. Italian army battalions
    B. German missiles
    C. The two atomic bombs dropped on Japan
    D. Nightclubs in Berlin

REVIEW & RESOURCES

48. Which Allied country's forces arrived in Berlin first?

    A.   The United States
    B.   Britain
    C.   France
    D.   The USSR

49. In the last six months of the war, what was the U.S. strategy for winning the conflict with Japan?

    A.   Negotiate with Japan for a conditional surrender
    B.   Insert ground forces on the Japanese home islands
    C.   Break the Japanese will with massive bombing raids on Japanese cities
    D.   Place all of Japan under a naval blockade until the country surrendered

50. At what conference did the Allies set the terms for the Japanese surrender?

    A.   The Yalta Conference
    B.   The Casablanca Conference
    C.   The Tehran Conference
    D.   The Potsdam Conference

Suggestions for Further Reading

BERGSTROM, CHRISTER, AND ANDREY MIKHAILOV. *Black Cross/Red Star: The Air War Over the Eastern Front.* Volume 1. Pacifica, California: Pacifica Military History, 2000.

GILBERT, MARTIN. *The Second World War: A Complete History.* Revised edition. New York: Henry Holt, 2004.

LOZA, DMITRIY. *Attack of the Airacobras: Soviet Aces, American P-39s, and the Air War Against Germany.* Lawrence: University Press of Kansas, 2002

MAY, ERNEST R. *Strange Victory: Hitler's Conquest of France.* New York: Hill and Wang, 2001.

SCHOM, ALAN. *The Eagle and the Rising Sun: The Japanese-American War 1941–1943.* New York: W. W. Norton, 2004.

STOKESBURY, JAMES L. *A Short History of World War II.* New York: William Morrow, 1980.

TOWNSEND, PETER. *Duel of Eagles.* New York: Barnes & Noble Books, 1970.

REVIEW & RESOURCES

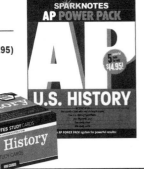